Princeton University

THE CAMPUS GUIDE

Princeton University

Raymond P. Rhinehart

With Photographs by Walter Smalling Jr.

Princeton Architectural Press

NEW YORK | *1999*

This book has been made possible through the generous support
of the Graham Foundation for Advanced Studies in the Fine Arts.

Princeton Architectural Press
37 East 7th Street
New York, NY 10003
212.995.9620

For a free catalog of other books published by Princeton Architectural Press,
call toll free 1.800.722.6657 or visit www.papress.com

Printed in Hong Kong
04 03 02 01 00 5 4 3 2 1 First Edition

Editing: Jan Cigliano
Design: Sara E. Stemen
Maps: Jane Garvie
Special thanks to Ann Alter, Eugenia Bell, Caroline Green, Beth Harrison, Clare Jacobson, Leslie Ann Kent, Mark Lamster, Anne Nitschke, Lottchen Shivers, and Jennifer Thompson of Princeton Architectural Press —Kevin C. Lippert, *publisher*

Library of Congress Cataloguing-in-Publication Data
Rhinehart, Raymond P., 1940–
The campus guide. Princeton University : an architectural tour / by Raymond P. Rhinehart ; with photographs by Walter Smalling Jr.
p. cm.
Includes bibliographical references (p.191) and index.
ISBN 1-56898-209-7 (pbk. : alk. paper)
1. Princeton University—Buildings. 2. Princeton University—Guidebooks. I. Title.
II. Title: Princeton University.
LD4611.R55 2000
378.749'65—dc21 99-29961
CIP

This above all: to thine own self be true,
And it must follow, as the night the day,
Thou canst not then be false to any man.
Polonius' advice to his son from Hamlet

How to use this book

This guide is intended for visitors, alumni, and students who wish to have an insider's look at the most historic and interesting buildings on Princeton University's campuses and around town, from Nassau Hall and Blair Arch on the main campus, to Princeton Graduate College, Princeton Theological Seminary, and the Institute for Advanced Study.

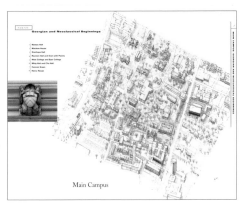

Main Campus

The book is divided into eleven Walks; each covers a specific precinct, or sub-area. Each Walk opens with a three-dimensional aerial map that locates the buildings on the walk, followed by an introductory essay of the area, and illustrated profiles of each building's history and architecture.

Included are works from the John B. Putnam Memorial Collection of twentieth-century sculpture, displayed throughout campus. The Putnam Collection honors an alumnus killed in air combat in 1944. Shortly before his death he wrote in his diary, "Courage is not the lack of fear but the ability to face it."

Campus Buildings open: 9:00AM–5:00PM Monday–Friday; closed holidays
Grounds open: dawn–dusk daily, year-round
Orange Key Tours, Maclean House: 10:00AM, 11:00AM, 1:30PM, 3:30PM daily, year-round. Admission: free. 609.258.3603
Parking Information: Public Safety office, Stanhope Hall; "Accessibility Guide" available 609.258.3157
University Bookstore open: 9:00AM–9:00PM daily 609.258.3647
Historical Society of Princeton, Bainbridge House, 158 Nassau Street: self-guided walking tours 609.258.3000

Further information:
    Princeton University
    Visitor Information Service
    Nassau Hall
    Princeton, NJ 08544
    609.258.6115
    www.princeton.edu

    Princeton Theological Seminary
    609.921.8300
    www.ptsem.edu

This guide is about the making and life of a special place, created by patrons and their architects. It plays off Corbusier's observation that American campuses are "green cities." Princeton is the consummate green city. Its density promotes the kind of accidental encounters and rhythms that are characteristic of a great city. Yet it also provides the green, the peaceful centering, the emotional experience of nature. As it has been created and evolved since 1753, Princeton caters to the whole man and woman. It is, therefore, the ideal city—a marketplace for ideas set in a garden.

McCosh Walk

The narrative of this guide is built on an assumption: architecture, especially the architecture where learning takes place, is more than a utilitarian shelter to accommodate human activity. Not only is architecture an expression of value, it also can be enlisted to shape values. How architecture reflects and how it shapes has tended to be re-cast by each generation that builds or occupies a structure. Given Princeton's 250-year history, the campus is an especially rich record of different answers to formative questions. Take nature, for example: the Georgian, neoclassic, Victorian, Collegiate Gothic, modern, and post-modern campuses exist like geological layers bearing clues to the shifting attitudes toward nature and landscape, first to be overcome as the American wilderness was being settled, then eventually brought back on a leash in carefully laid out and clipped gardens. Which is to say this guide attempts to go beyond architecture as stageset design; it seeks to get below the surface to explore what seems to be shaping an individual building or an entire precinct of the campus.

There are definitely heroes and, if not villains, at least such negative forces as a lack of vision, expediency, and imagination. If there is one figure who towers above the rest, it is James McCosh. McCosh arrived on the campus of a sleepy, drifting college in 1868, grabbed it by the scruff of the neck, shook it, and set it on the course to become a great university. His success argues that history is often written by the will of visionary, persuasive, and passionate men and women. There are others: President John Witherspoon, 1768–1794, who also signed the Declaration of Independence; Andrew Fleming West, the first dean of the Graduate College, 1901–1928; President Woodrow Wilson, 1902–1910; and Ralph Adams Cram, supervising architect and high priest of the the Collegiate Gothic style during 1907–1929, who worked in concert with the great landscape gardener Beatrix Farrand, 1912–1943,who elevated landscape gardening to an art and bequeathed to Princeton a legacy of beauty second to no other American campus. The intellectual and imaginative heat generated by these individuals was literally transformational.

But this guide does not confine itself to Princeton University's undergraduate campus and Princeton's Graduate College. Included are Walks around sister institutions—the Princeton Theological Seminary and the Institute for Advanced Study. Both the seminary and the institute share history with the university. Often it is seen in the architecture. Nassau Hall has its equivalent in the seminary's Alexander Hall and the institute's Fuld Hall. The latter two are nineteenth- and twentieth-century reinterpretations of Nassau Hall. The different paths the seminary and the institute eventually took throw light back on what is distinctive about today's university. The seminary's historic core recalls the essence of Princeton's Victorian campus, while the institute embraced modernism more readily than the university.

An understanding and appreciation of the university are further advanced by at least an introduction to the near vicinity of Princeton Borough. Therefore, the final walk centers on Nassau Street and the imme-diate neighborhood of Princeton's Main Street.

The university, the graduate college, the seminary, the institute, and the town itself are the warp and weft of an extraordinary architectural tapes-try, which this guide seeks to identify, respond to, and often celebrate. Ironically, Princeton University's uniqueness threatens this precious legacy. It is a legacy that could easily be embraced to death by commercial and private interests eager to acquire a piece of history. The guide is thus written for those who are in the best positions to preserve and build constructively on this legacy: the alumni and parents of the three institutions, the administra-tions, the students and their professors, Princeton residents, and visitors from this country and abroad who come to this special place.

Why does everyone love the Princeton campus and why is it uniquely distinguished as a setting for institutional life? We think one reason is that the architecture of the University is both good and varied, in its generic manifestations—Georgian, Tuscan Villa, Ruskinian Gothic, Collegiate Gothic and Modern—and in its easy and harmonious evolutions over time combining analogous and contrasting relationships among buildings and styles.

Another reason is that the spaces between buildings on this campus are unified and artfully pedestrian in quality and scale, as they have evolved in time from space punctuated by buildings, in early decades, to space directed or enclosed by buildings in later years.

Campus planning at Princeton has historically balanced two approaches. The first, in the original Nassau Hall complex, engages unifying axes and symmetries among classical forms seen as fixed points in space; the second, in the Rockefeller-Mathey College complex, employs picturesque and continuous forms to direct and enclose space and is perceived as evolving over time. Both ways are loved by Princetonians. Each richly acknowledges and tensely juxtaposes the ideal and the pragmatic, the classical and the Romantic, the formal and the picturesque. Most important, in the history of the planning of the Princeton campus the various combinings of these two ways have been directed pragmatically rather than grandiosely. This has made the campus plan incomplete yet ironically whole at any one time.

Balances have consistently evolved as well between growth via expansion at the edges of the campus and growth by infill within the fabric of the campus—and between attention to the whole (not domineering) and to the details (not fussy).

While Princeton's configurations of space, form, and symbol enhance the aura of the campus, their generic architecture works too to accommodate decades of changing institutional programs. The way in which connections were established between built form and educational policy over the years as the Princeton campus was constructed has been brilliantly analyzed by the Princeton historian Donald Drew Egbert, in *The Modern Princeton* (Princeton University Press, 1947).

Egbert dwelled on the symbolic content of the architecture intended to embody philosophic and pedagogical aspirations. He referred as well to the cycle of taste where we tend to react against the architecture of the recent past and to like that of a generation earlier. Egbert's view suggests we practice tolerance as we evaluate recent architecture—remember Alexander Hall was despised when we were young.

Robert Venturi and Denise Scott Brown
October 29, 1999

Georgian and Neoclassical Beginnings

Main Campus

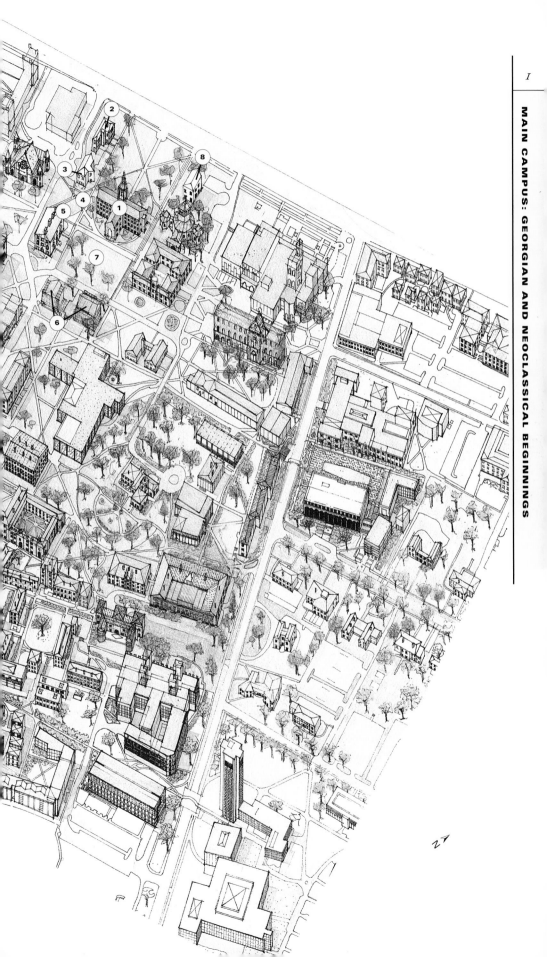

The Beginnings: 1746–1865

NH connection

Meeting in Newark in 1753, the trustees of the College of New Jersey were at a fateful crossroads. The college, which had been founded in Elizabeth in 1746, was debating yet another move. The debate was prompted by religious and economic considerations. But there was another issue that weighed heavily on their minds. To a man, the trustees of the fledgling college believed there was a close relationship between environment and human conduct. The right environment would nurture a young mind and encourage the growth of a godly spirit; the wrong place could corrupt it.

The borough of Princeton answered the call in two ways. First, the trustees were among the evangelical Presbyterians—the so-called "New Light"—who were establishing Protestant churches throughout the British-American colonies at a fast pace and increasingly needed qualified ministers to tend to the spiritual needs of the growing flock. They needed an institution of their own to train young men to take the word deep into the wilderness. It would be an expensive undertaking and the trustees required that the chosen community donate land and wooded lots for fuel and building materials to help underwrite the cost. Several communities expressed interest, but it was the citizens of the borough of Princeton who came forward. Its selection seems almost preordained. The trustees were eager for a site, according to Princeton president and trustee Aaron Burr Sr., "more sequestered from the various temptations attending a promiscuous converse with the world, that theatre of folly and dissipation." The small town of Princeton came up with the required land and wood; the absence of urban folly and dissipation was a distinct plus.

Yet it was also an odd site, a small collection of buildings half way between Philadelphia and New York. Hardly more than a change of horses on the well-traveled mud rut that was rather grandly called the King's Highway. In retrospect, it seems improbable that one of America's preeminent universities would be located in this isolated place. Even more improbable, on the day Nassau Hall opened its doors in 1756, it was the largest building in the colonies—and it stood in an open field. From the perspective of two-and-a-half centuries later, Nassau's siting would be like finding the Empire State Building on the high plains of Wyoming

Unlike Harvard, William and Mary, and Yale, which were developed as part of urban fabrics, the College of New Jersey put down its roots in country soil. Stepping back a considerable distance from the King's Highway like a great plantation manor house, Nassau Hall was designed to be approached by way of a large lawn or green that gradually rose toward the south. In donating this particular four-and-a-half acres to the college, the FitzRandolph family enabled the new school to take command of one of the higher elevations in the area from which the land fell off to the north and south, thus affording commanding views. This preoccupation with views and vistas has guided the future development of the university, right down to the present day.

There was another element that shaped the development of the campus, one more subtle but finally no less profound—the openness of the land itself. Occupying the middle distance between what is today Nassau Street and Nassau Hall, the intervening green is more than a neutral area between town and college; it is the open space, the campus, the collegial center that holds the two elements in balance. Perhaps it is not surprising that the current use of the term *campus,* a Latin word, had its origin at Princeton around 1770. The fact that an ancient word has been adopted by most American institutions of higher learning suggests that the term succinctly embraces a wide range of ideas and principles first articulated at Princeton.

If the vistas direct one's line of sight out into the world, and if the openness of the land provides an emotional centering, the architecture offers the contrary dimension of enclosure. As the mediator between man and nature, architecture also reflects complex and shifting attitudes toward privacy, community, nature, ambition, and purpose. A stageset for nearly three centuries to succeeding waves of enlightenment, religious revival, romantic introspection, imperial pretension, and scientific rationalism, the architecture of the university articulates and embraces the tensions in all our lives. There is in most of us the rationalist, the dreamy romantic, the democrat, the elitist, the poet, and the scientist. Unlike many post-World War II master-planned campuses that follow a uniform vision, Princeton's architecture reflects many-sided views across 250 years about the place of man in the scheme of things. A walk through the campus brings forth lively conversations and competing voices about the buildings. Outside the Public Safety Office at Stanhope Hall, for example, the campus guard is still critical of the tearing down over a century ago of Philosophical Hall, the mate to Stanhope, that faced it to the front and east of Nassau Hall. "If it were still standing, the campus would have looked more like Harvard," he claims. And there is the alumnus who writes to the *Princeton Alumni Weekly*: "If I had $500 million to spare, I would give it all to Princeton with but one unbreakable string attached: the money would have to be used, first, to raze every campus building erected after, say, 1950."

Passions run deep. What keeps the debate civil is the larger design that accommodates, if not embraces, all sides. The story of Princeton's undergraduate main campus is not about any one extraordinary building. There are no heroes or box office stars here. There is a great ensemble, a whole that is greater than the sum of its parts. Despite changes in architectural fashion and educational curriculum, the university has sustained over the centuries a nearly unwavering commitment to vistas, open space, and enclosures (or outdoor rooms). Importantly, there is an uncompromising investment in proximity: no undergraduate student has to walk more than ten minutes to get to class.

An architectural walk around the upper and oldest precinct of the campus is made up of three, expanding circles, each beginning at or near Nassau Hall—the magnetic north of the university if not the entire Princeton community. The three walks have something of the character of a geological excavation, the oldest layer beginning at Nassau Hall. Not surprisingly, the original fabric of the earliest Georgian and neoclassical buildings is least intact as the university has grown over the years and adopted new forms in response to a changing world. Nevertheless much remains. In part because Princeton's prevailing spirit is conservative, and in part because it is also frugal, more likely to recycle or even move an entire building rather than tear it down. Henry House, originally built in 1837 and today standing northeast of Nassau Hall, has occupied four sites on campus and each time it was moved very carefully, as if it were a well-loved piece of furniture in a living room.

1. Nassau Hall   *Robert Smith and William Shippen, 1756*

National Historic Landmark

> The greatest danger will be over-building themselves, by attempting a large house in the beginning, sufficient to contain the whole institution. Large houses are always ugly, inconvenient, exposed to the accident of fire, and bad in cases of infection. A plain small house for the school and lodging of each professor is best. These connected by covered ways out of which the rooms of the students should open would be best. These may be built only as they shall be wanting. In fact a university should not be a house, but a village.
>
> —Thomas Jefferson to L. W. Tazwell, January 5, 1805

There is no direct evidence Thomas Jefferson had Nassau Hall in mind when he criticized the practice of squeezing an entire college into a single "large house." But he would have certainly known about the College. After all, in 1777 Princeton was the site of the first major victory in the Colonists'

Nassau Hall, left; *Maclean or President's House,* right (engraving by Henry Dakins, 1764)

fight for independence, and in 1783 Nassau Hall hosted the Continental Congress, after members fled Philadelphia in the face of their own mutinous soldiers.

Jefferson may have been promoting his own ideas of what a college should look like, but he did have a point. Forcing students, teachers, and the administration to live and work in the confines of one large building invited trouble. Ringing bells at all hours of the night or rolling cannon balls down the entire length of the long, dark halls were favorite student pranks that exhausted the patience of more than one sober cleric. But discipline was not the only problem. Just as Jefferson had predicted, the long halls also promoted the spread of disease and devastating fires.

Flaws notwithstanding, when Nassau Hall opened its doors in 1756, it was an overnight sensation. It was the largest building in the Colonies— capable of housing 150 students and their teachers—and one of the most admired and imitated. War, conflagration, and the work of succeeding generations of architects have pounded its walls. But those walls have held, a testament to the skill of its builders, both those who set the stone and those who planted the seeds of a great university.

When Edward Shippen arrived in Newark on January 24, 1753, he was prepared to discuss with his fellow trustees how the College of New Jersey was to be housed in its new Princeton home. The plans he carried called for a structure 190 feet long and 50 feet deep. Although the original documents do not survive, they appear to have been based on a design sketched in Philadelphia by Shippen's brother, Dr. William Shippen, in collaboration with Robert Smith (1722–1777). Smith was not an architect. He lived in an era before there was a formal profession. Instead, he was a gifted representative of a type of practical artist called a carpenter-builder. Born in Dalkeith, near Edinburgh, Scotland, Smith apprenticed to a builder and may have worked for the great Scottish designer William Adam. In this immigrant carpenter-builder, the trustees found their man, for he gave them a building and a level of craftsmanship that, figuratively and literally, put the new college on the map.

The art of architecture is no stranger to compromise. After all, someone else typically pays the bills. The Nassau Hall that was constructed was not quite the building Smith had in mind. He had recommended brick walls: brick was easier to handle, and Smith believed that a manufactured building product communicated a

Nassau Hall, faculty room

message of quality. But brick was also expensive, which for the strict Presbyterians definitely was not a sign of Godliness. So it fell to a local mason named William Worth to suggest a less costly alternative—the local metamorphic rock or gneiss, which Worth quarried from a site on the south bank of what today is Lake Carnegie. Since then, the rich honey-colored local stone with its sparkling flecks of mica has been quarried again and again for additional buildings, especially the dormitories. Over the years, the tonality and texture of this stone has tied together visually much of the campus and has given Princeton a definite look and sense of place. The local stone has also become a symbol of the powerful idea that had established the College of New Jersey in the first place: like the university, the twenty-six-inch-thick walls of Nassau Hall seem capable of handling everything man and nature can throw at them.

But neither the university nor Nassau Hall has remained unchanged, and that, too, is a symbol of life and the capacity to grow. Thus the Nassau Hall we see today is significantly different from the building that first opened its doors to regular classes. Echoing the prevailing architectural style of the mid eighteenth century, Smith had designed a Georgian plan and elevation. To say "Georgian" means an obsession for symmetry: what is on the left side of the front door is repeated on the right, both inside the building and out. Also typical of Georgian architecture, the windows, entrances, and the very edges of the structure are clearly articulated and proportional to one another. But a century after it was built, the Georgian bones of Nassau Hall were wrapped in Victorian clothes.

The three-story plus English basement structure we see today, with its hipped roof, belfry, and central projecting gabled pavilions at the north and south facades, are true in plan to Smith's design but not in detail. The massive walls of warm ochre-hued stone likewise remain, covered in many places with ivy planted by succeeding graduating classes since 1870. But the original three front doorways with flat arches and stone quoins, each approached by a flight of stairs, are gone.

The back, or south, elevation has been changed. Originally there were two doors on axis to the east and west entries at the front. These rear openings would have been more like service doors, providing egress to, among other things, privies. Today the rear entrances are gone. Another change: the south pavilion did not extend nearly so far as it does today. In fact, the north and south pavilions at the center of the building were roughly of the same size, in keeping with the rigidly symmetrical character of the original Georgian design. The expansion of the rear pavilion came a century later when the way in which the interior space was used changed radically.

The seeming efficiency of having all functions under one roof made Nassau Hall a model for colleges then being founded up and down the Eastern seaboard and beyond, including Brown, Dartmouth, Rutgers, and the University of South Carolina. In fact, Nassau Hall influenced collegiate architecture well into the nineteenth century, as can be seen just down the street at Princeton Theological Seminary's Alexander Hall (1815).

What were the sources for Smith's design? Princeton historian T. J. Wertenbaker, in *Princeton 1746–1896* (1946), points to the contemporary pattern books that builders and carpenters regularly consulted, in particular Batty Langley's *Builder's Treasury of Designs* or Gibbs's *A Book of Architecture*: "If we remove the 'superfluous ornaments' (President Aaron Burr Senior's characterization) from Gibbs's design for King's College, Cambridge, we have a close approach to Nassau Hall—the proportions, the hipped roof, the central facade topped by a pediment, the ornamental urns. The central doorway, with a head of Homer dominating the flat arch, clearly was borrowed from Langley's *Treasury of Designs*, while the cupola is a replica of the upper part of the cupola of St. Mary-le-Strand, London, shown in Gibbs's book."

The sources Smith may have consulted are less important than the larger point of what the trustees were telling the world. By turning to current fashion and by building on such a massive scale, they announced that the evangelical wing of the Presbyterian Church and with it the College of New Jersey were here to stay. Nor were the trustees averse to an extra bit of insurance: they immediately picked up on the suggestion of New Jersey's Royal Governor Jonathan Belcher (1747–1757) to name their first and major building after the late and highly esteemed King William (1689–1702) of the Dutch House of Nassau-Orange.

A venerable name and size notwithstanding, life in Nassau Hall was Spartan. As President Burr wrote to a Scots donor: "We do everything in the plainest and cheapest manner, as far as is consistent with Decency and Convenience, having no superfluous Ornaments." It is no small irony that over the years Princeton has gained a reputation as the university of choice for families of affluence and standing. Certainly that was not the intent of its stern Scots founders for whom "cheap" was not something to be ashamed of, but a decided virtue.

2. Maclean House   *Robert Smith, 1756*

National Historic Landmark

One other fragment of the university's eighteenth-century history remains in Maclean House. For many years Maclean was the official residence of the college president, thus its earlier name, "President's House." Today Maclean is the home of the Alumni Council. The house takes its name from John Maclean Jr., vice president and president of Princeton, 1854–1868. President Maclean was the genius behind the creation in 1826 of the Alumni Association, which in subsequent years has played a decisive role in

Maclean House

securing Princeton's financial stability. Evidence of Maclean's genius was his ability to convince a former U. S. President, James Madison (class of 1771), to become its first president. From this auspicious beginning, the alumni association grew in stature to became an influential counterweight to an often reactionary board of trustees dominated by Presbyterian ministers.

But what about the architecture of the building? This time the architect was able to use brick. President Aaron Burr Sr. (1748–1757), was the first in a succession of chief executives who for over a hundred years called this modest house on the town's main street home. During this time, Maclean House was significantly altered: the roof was raised, dormers inserted, a front porch attached, and two bays added on the east and west sides. Also, the brick was painted yellow. Before the addition of the front porch and side bays, the house was basically a simple rectangle, except for the rear stair tower. Placing the stairs at the rear allowed for a spacious center hall. Unlike the interior of Nassau Hall, where none of the original fabric survives, Maclean is relatively intact. The finishes, raised paneling, a turned balustrade on the stair, and a fluted arch in the hall confirm that Smith was a gifted carpenter.

Visitors to the Princeton campus typically make Maclean House their first stop, since it is the headquarters of the student Orange Key Guide Service, which is located toward the back at the southwest corner of the house. The garden behind Maclean House is a gift of the class of 1936. Although the first occupants would most likely have planted vegetables—if anything—this garden is ornamental and meant to suggest an eighteenth-century garden. The flowers and shrubs come from the grounds of Mt. Vernon. On the other side of the house, in the front lawn near Nassau Street stand two gnarled sycamores. Almost as old as the house itself, the trees are commonly known as the "Stamp Act Sycamores," having allegedly been planted in 1765 to commemorate the repeal of the Stamp Act. The facts do not support the legend, but it makes a good story. For a campus justifiably renowned for its landscaping, it comes as a surprise to learn that these two sycamores may have been the only trees planted on campus until the early nineteenth century.

After the President's House and Nassau Hall, nothing else of consequence was built on campus until the first decade of the nineteenth century. This pause was a result of the disruption brought on by the Revolutionary War, a conflict in which both the town and the College had a front seat. However, the price of being part of history did not come cheap: there was severe damage to buildings throughout the area, especially Nassau Hall, which was abused by troops of both sides. It took nearly twenty years before the College was compensated for the damage by state and national governments.

Success was brief. Shortly after the repairs had been completed, Nassau Hall was gutted by fire in 1802. The trustees immediately embarked on a fund-raising campaign to rebuild. Their efforts were so successful that the College was able to undertake an ambitious building campaign that went beyond Nassau Hall. The man in charge was the Philadelphia architect Benjamin Henry Latrobe (1764–1820).

Born and educated in England, Latrobe moved in 1798 to Philadelphia, where he worked as the first professionally trained architect in the United States. The same fire that led to his being hired to restore Nassau Hall gave him the opportunity to design two additional structures that faced one another, rather than the street. Sited at the northeast and northwest corners of Nassau Hall, both buildings were the first decisive move toward a major reorientation of the campus to conform to a symmetrical, neoclassical plan.

3. Stanhope Hall *Benjamin Henry Latrobe, 1803*

Stanhope Hall

Stanhope is the only one of Latrobe's two new buildings to have survived. Originally called Geological Hall, the building was later named for Princeton's seventh President, Samuel Stanhope Smith (1795–1812), who served as acting President during the years when President John Witherspoon (1768–1794) was an active member of the Continental Congress. Its mate, Philosophical Hall, which stood opposite to the east, was Stanhope's mirror image in every detail—arched windows, central pavilions, strong pediments, and of course the rich aubergines and ochres of the local Stockton sandstone. The practice of designing paired or matching buildings was an additional neoclassical trait, repeated again and again in the next thirty years of Princeton's growth. Philosophical Hall contained the kitchen, dining hall, a room for the "philosophical" apparatus (or, scientific equipment), recitation rooms for classes in mathematics and natural philosophy, and an observatory. Neither a victim of fire or war, Philosophical Hall was torn down in the early 1870s to make way for the college's first free-standing library, Chancellor Green Hall.

Its surviving twin has a distinguished history. Originally the home of the Princeton's book collection and its debating and literary societies—the American Whig and the Cliosophic—as well as study halls for freshmen and sophomores, Stanhope today houses the university's Communications and the Public Safety Offices. Of additional interest to visitors is the availability of public restrooms, which is to say little of Latrobe's original interior survives.

With the Victorianized outline of Nassau Hall to one side and the kaleidoscopic octagonals of Chancellor Green Hall across the way, Stanhope looks isolated and adrift. It relates to nothing else in the vicinity apart from being built from the same stone as Nassau Hall. The impression of isolation is justified: Stanhope is in fact a fragment. To appreciate fully the impact it would have had when it was built, Stanhope has to be seen as the surviving element of a three-piece ensemble: Latrobe's remodeled Nassau Hall in the middle and Stanhope Hall and Philosophical Hall as arms or pavilions.

4. Reunion Hall and Oval with Points

Reunion Hall   *1870*
Oval with Points   *Henry Moore, sculptor, 1969–1970*

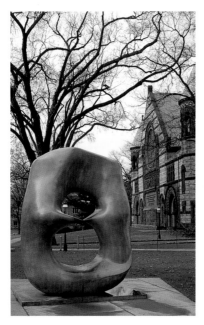

Oval with Points by Henry Moore

Between Stanhope and West College there used to stand a dormitory, Reunion Hall, demolished in 1966. Built in 1870, Reunion celebrated the reconciliation of two factions of the Presbyterian Church. The dormitory had one other claim to fame: A future President of the United States roomed here during the first semester of his freshman year (1935), until a physician advised the young Jack Kennedy to take it easy and transfer to Harvard— or so student folklore would have it.

Where Reunion stood there is now an abstract bronze, *Oval with Points*, by British sculptor Henry Moore (1898–1986). One of many works of art sited around the campus as part of the John B. Putnam Jr. Memorial Collection of twentieth-century sculpture, Moore's piece may be nothing more or less than an abstract composition, although the shape—an oval the midsections of which seem to be bending to join one another— does suggest the concept of union or reunion. Students have their own interpretation of the shape. They point out that by standing back from the sculpture at a certain distance and at a certain angle, the silhouette can be plausibly described as "Nixon's nose."

5. West College and East College

West College *John Notman, 1836; remodeled and expanded, Aymar Embury, 1926*
East College *John Notman, 1836; demolished, 1896*

West College

Like Stanhope, West College is also a fragment. Originally built as one of a pair of identical opposed dormitories and for some time the home of the university store, West College is currently used for offices, including those of undergraduate admissions, the dean of the College, the dean of students, the registrar, undergraduate financial aid, and student employment. Built at a cost of $13,000, West College was designed to be 112 feet long and 32 feet wide with eight suites on each floor. (It ended up being 22 feet shorter). Along with East College, its long-since demolished companion, West College was among Princeton's first structures specifically built to house its growing student population. The designs of East and West followed strict guidelines laid down by the trustees, including the size, building material, and siting, which, thanks to the bad experience of Nassau Hall, was deliberately oriented to catch the prevailing westerly breezes.

Like Nassau Hall, the silhouette of West College has been reshaped by changing needs and fashion. Perhaps inspired by Reunion Hall, both West College and East College underwent Victorian re-roofing projects that gave both a mansard hat. Practical as well as stylish, the steep slope of the new roofs transformed the attics into useful living space. Six decades later, West College was remodeled and expanded on its west side in a Colonial Revival style by Aymar Embury (1880–1966), a Princeton alumnus. In a move that restored the original structure to an approximation of its original shape, the roof was again altered and lowered to its present height. Embury was a favorite of the power brokers who shaped public works projects in New York and on Long Island from the 1920s into the 1960s. His own favorite, the Bronx-Whitestone Bridge, is arguably his most famous design.

6. Whig Hall and Clio Hall

Charles Steadman, 1838; remodeled and moved, A. Page Brown, 1893

South and east of West College stand two pristine Greek temples. Until the end of the Civil War, both defined the southern boundary of the Princeton campus. Whig and Clio represent the final chapter in an episode begun by Latrobe that saw the growth of the College along the symmetrical outline of a neoclassic quadrangle. The rhythm established to the north by Stanhope

Whig Hall

Whig Hall, left; *Clio Hall*, right

and Philosophical Halls, which was continued by East and West Colleges, was completed in 1838 by yet another set of essentially duplicate buildings, only in this case they do not face one another, but turn ninety degrees and look back to the south elevation of Nassau Hall.

At the time of their completion, a pedestrian standing on Nassau Street who looked south into the campus would have seen that Whig and Clio were the terminus of parallel walks that ran past the east and west sides of Nassau Hall. This is not the view one sees today. The seemingly timeless serenity of Whig and Clio belies what is in fact a complex history. Although the buildings we see accurately mimic the design of the original structures, neither is the same size or constructed of the same material as the original. Indeed, neither stands quite in the same place.

Although the story of the American Whig and Cliosophic Societies (1769 and 1770 respectively) reaches back to the 18th century, their importance in the life of the college was most fully felt in the century that followed, the first decades of which were a period of great student unrest. Much of that unrest was directed toward reforming the curriculum, which the students increasingly believed was no longer relevant to their world. Finding little support among the faculty and even less among the trustees, the students took on the challenge themselves. Their resource was the two rival literary and debating societies.

Both organizations provided not only needed opportunities for social interaction, they also offered an alternative curriculum. Here, students could acquire the communications skills so important to nineteenth century politics, commerce, and religion—not to mention the social networking that continued long after school. Further, the libraries of both societies were a much needed supplement to the meager resources of the College's library, which did not have its own free-standing building until 1873. In short, Whig and Clio were part fraternity, part athletic club, and part student union. Their attraction was only heightened by the fact that membership was a closely held secret, so secret that the front doors had combination locks that only the members could open.

Housed in Stanhope in the early decades of the nineteenth century, both societies eventually required separate free-standing structures. In 1835 the Cliosophic Society formed a building committee, which commissioned the highly regarded carpenter-architect Charles Steadman (1790–1868) to buy a design from distinguished Philadelphia architect John Haviland (1792–1852). At the time, this was a common way of doing business. Haviland sent back the specifications for a classical edifice modeled after the Greek temple of Teos. More classically eclectic than archeologically precise, Haviland turned to the temple on the Ilissus for the Ionic capitals that grace the six columns supporting the pediment. Steadman's work was so well received that he was asked to provide the Whig Society with a copy located to the east of Clio. Both structures were paid for by their respective societies, not by the College, which no doubt dictated the use of inexpensive building materials—wood, stucco, brick, and a lot of white paint. A potential fire hazard and always in need of repair, both structures were from the beginning candidates for a major remake.

Conventional wisdom has it that what finally prompted the remake was not fire but the declining fortunes of both societies that occurred in the later decades of the nineteenth century. Perhaps motivated in part by concern over the rise of the decidedly unintellectual upperclass Eating Clubs, the College intervened by commissioning the architect A. Page Brown (1859–1896) to house both organizations in more stately mansions. Brown certainly had the credentials to give the job a touch of class, since he had received his training at McKim, Mead and White, one of the leading firms of the day. Clearly both the College and the architect believed that the reputation of Whig and Clio would be invigorated by elevating their status through the medium of a grander design. Like the Roman Emperor Augustus before him, where Brown found brick and stucco, he left marble in its place.

Both of the original buildings were torn down in 1889 and were replaced by the present structures. What had been wood and stucco is now slabs of marble two inches thick. Likewise, the original modest wood columns were replaced by solid marble copies, twenty feet high and three feet in diameter. Inside, Brown designed libraries, reading rooms, club rooms, and on the third floors spacious senate chambers. Brown also moved Whig and Clio closer to one another. This was not an arbitrary gesture. In the final decade of the nineteenth century, Whig and Clio no longer defined the southern edge of the campus. It thus made sense to move them out of the way of an expanded line of sight from the north of Nassau Hall that could now flow uninterrupted south

As Princeton alumnus F. Scott Fitzgerald has written, in America there are no second acts. Undoubtedly impressive and rich in their historic connotations, Whig and Clio nevertheless continued their decline. The center of gravity of Princeton's social life had irrevocably moved east to Prospect Avenue and the Eating Clubs.

There is a postscript. As a result of a 1969 fire that gutted the interior and east wall, Whig underwent a dramatic redesign by the New York firm of Gwathmey and Siegel (1972), for which the firm received an American Institute of Architects Honor Award. The interior auditorium, meeting rooms, the semi-attached circular elevator tower at the rear for handicap access, and other amenities are in a thoroughly modernist vein. By removing the solid east wall and deeply carving into the resulting imaginary plane to reveal a glassed-in cross section of the interior spaces, the architects undoubtedly create a more dramatic experience of the building, especially at night when it glows like a lantern.

7. Cannon Green

Cannon Green

It is difficult to imagine that until well into the nineteenth century, organized sports were often actively discouraged as unmanly (!) and frivolous. This opinion was by no means unique to Princeton. But what man decrees, nature eventually overcomes. And so it came to pass that at Princeton, Cannon Green became the place where students worked off their energy in unsupervised play. The tree-shaded open green space between Whig/Clio and Nassau Halls takes its name from the large cannon at the center whose muzzle is deeply buried into the ground.

A relic of the Revolutionary battles in and around Princeton, the cannon had been hauled to New Brunswick to defend the city during the War of 1812. Over the years as it lay marooned in New Brunswick, it became an object of contention between Princeton and Rutgers. Retrieved in 1835 by a posse of Princeton citizens and students led by Winston Churchill's grandfather, the peripatetic cannon at last came to rest in its present position in 1840. The largest trees on Cannon Green, some of which are up to five feet in diameter, are white ash. It seems likely the trees were planted in 1836 when Joseph Henry laid out the grounds. No longer the physical center of the campus, Cannon Green remains Princeton's historic and spiritual heart.

8. Henry House *Joseph Henry, 1837*

Henry House

In a community distinguished by a long history of relocating buildings rather than tearing them down, Henry House makes the mobility of Dorothy's air-borne house in the *Wizard of Oz* seem positively leaden. Henry House began its history on a site to the west of Nassau Hall between Stanhope Hall and West College. The construction of Reunion Hall in 1870 caused it to be moved to a location where the University Chapel now stands. When the Chapel was constructed in 1925, Henry House was moved a short distance to the north to a site that would eventually accommodate Firestone Library. When it came the turn for Firestone Library to be built in 1947, Henry House was picked up and transported to its current site to the north and east of Nassau Hall. Along the way, a number of restorations has considerably altered the exterior ornament. The wing to the north and the porch on the south are additions to Henry's quietly elegant Federal design centered by a pilaster-framed entrance that is pierced by a simple fanlight and sidelights. Like Alumni House across the way, the brick has been painted yellow.

Besides being an obviously capable amateur architect, a subject which he taught as an elective, Joseph Henry (1797–1878) established Princeton's reputation as a leader in the study of physics. His experiments with the telegraph, which included stringing a wire between his office in Philosophical Hall and his house, predate those of Morse. (It was a convenient way for Henry to let his household know he was about to come over for lunch.) A veritable Renaissance man, it was Henry who in 1836 created the first written master plan for the future growth of the campus.

Three decades earlier Latrobe had provided a model for how future buildings should be placed on campus. Henry took his lead from Latrobe's initial gesture and drew a plan for the entire College. Like his own house, the campus would reflect the neoclassical ideals of balance, symmetry, clarity, and simple geometric forms. It was Henry who selected the sites for Whig and Clio Halls. Henry's reputation was such that he was lured away from Princeton in 1846 to assume a national position as the first director and secretary of the Smithsonian Institution. By that time, a new spirit was in the air that would profoundly reorient the plan of the campus and the individual buildings themselves away from the calculated symmetry of the rational to the equally calculated spontaneity of the romantic.

The Victorian Campus

Main Campus

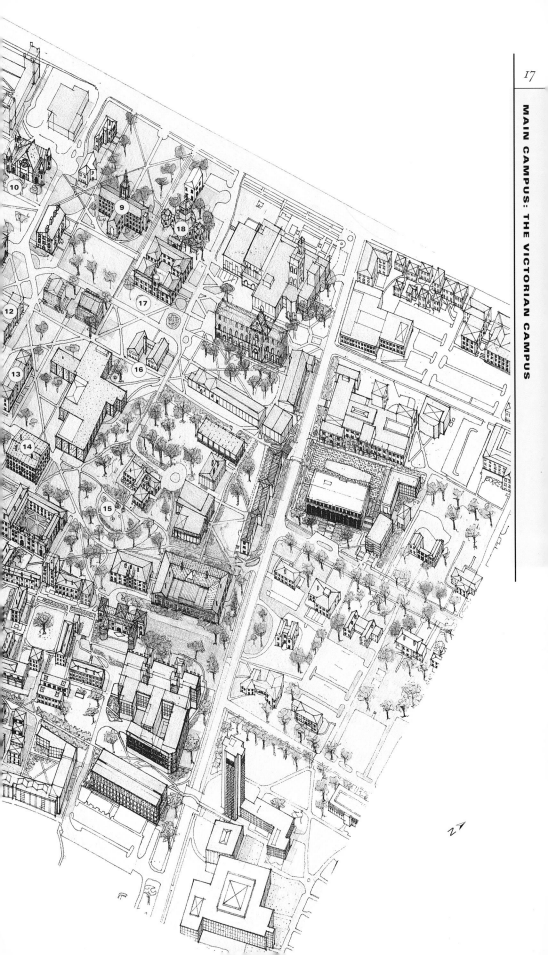

> It is unfortunate that the greatest era of college expansion in the United States should have coincided with a period of poor architectural taste. Not only at Princeton but at scores of other colleges, early American traditions were discarded in favor of ornate towers, steep roofs set off by varicolored slate, broken facades and Romanesque doors and windows.
>
> Thomas Jefferson Wertenbaker, *Princeton 1746–1896*

Besides illustrating the shifting nature of taste, Wertenbaker's words point up the risk you take when you criticize your parents. Certainly from our perspective several generations later, the exuberant Victorian legacy is one of the treasures of the Princeton campus. No other period comes close to the intoxication Victorians had when handling building materials—granite, marble, limestone, brownstone, redstone, slate in all its colors, tile, brick, terra-cotta, and so forth. If it could be quarried or forged, the Victorians wanted it polished, chiseled, rusticated, carved, and served up in great helpings to delight the eye and hand. Often all on the same building. But there was always method in the seeming madness.

Like the buildings of Princeton's Georgian and neoclassical periods, which are best understood as elements of a larger concept or plan, Princeton's Victorian campus also reveals a larger, albeit different, way of organizing separate elements into a coherent whole. However, rather than a rigorously symmetrical, formal pattern that emphasizes squares, rectangles, straight lines, and symmetry, a new organic architecture is set within what commentators refer to as a "pleasure garden." It is the difference between eighteenth-century Newtonian physics, which seeks unchanging, immutable laws of nature, and Darwinian biology with its emphasis on the evolutionary growth of the species. Great Victorian landscape architects, such as Andrew Downing and Frederick Law Olmsted, were the high priests of the oblique angle and the curved walk that constantly revealed surprises. But the genius behind the College's new direction was the gifted Scottish educator who came to Princeton in 1868 as its eleventh president, James McCosh (1811–1894). More than any other person, McCosh is the decisive force behind the evolution of the Princeton campus.

Struck by its relative barrenness, McCosh immediately set out to transform the grounds of the college into an English nobleman's park, which he regarded as "the highest model of landscape gardening." It was McCosh who persuaded the trustees to retain the services of a landscape gardener "to furnish a plan for the improvement of the College." That was an extraordinary change in direction; just how extraordinary can be gauged by trying to edit out in the mind's eye every bit of the present-day landscaping, except for the grass and a few trees. It is just not Princeton. The Princeton we see today began with McCosh who, along with his wife Isabella, would walk around the campus with cuttings tucked underneath his arm, always in search of another spot where nature assisted by the hand of man would reveal yet another delight. It was no idle boast when McCosh told a visitor, "It's me college. I made it."

9. Nassau Hall and Memorial Hall

Nassau Hall   *John Notman, 1855*
Nassau Hall, Faculty Room   *Raleigh C. Gildersleeve, 1906*
Memorial Hall   *Day and Klauder, 1919*

In Walk One our encounter with Nassau Hall on the Main Campus was with its Georgian and neoclassical ancestors. Although these voices can still be heard, Nassau Hall today is a Yankee wearing Florentine cloth cut by a Victorian tailor. The fabric doesn't quite fit the lanky bones, but the effect is nevertheless engaging because of the unique figure he cuts.

Just as the fire at the beginning of the century was an invitation for Latrobe to reshape Nassau Hall along neoclassical lines, a second disastrous fire in 1855 was yet another opportunity. For the third time, the college turned to a Philadelphia architect, John Notman (1810–1870), designer of Philadelphia's St. Mark's, the Church of the Holy Trinity, and many residences, including Prospect house on the Princeton campus. Notman's objectives were threefold: to repair quickly a vital piece of the campus fabric; to upgrade the structure to state-of-the-art fireproof construction; and to give Nassau the beauty appropriate to its prestige. For Notman, that meant converting it into an Italianate villa.

Notman was a devotee of the Florentine school popular in the fifth and sixth decade of the century. Queen Victoria's palace, "Osborne," had set the style, after which square towers, stone balconies, rounded arches of

Nassau Hall, 1840. Lithograph by John H. Bufford

Nassau Hall, circa 1860. Lithograph by F. Childs

doors and windows, and low roofs with deep, overhanging eaves became fashionable motifs for the well-heeled in England and America. Notman removed the existing north and south entrances of the original building and replaced these with square stair towers on the east and west sides. No doubt the alteration was made as much for reasons of fire safety as fashion. Notman's flanking stone towers rose a full story above the original roof, like massive bookends between which sat Smith's Georgian structure. Safety and fashion notwithstanding, these somewhat awkward "pepper pots" never won many converts. In the early years of the twentieth century, the tops of Notman's towers were lopped off by decree of the trustees.

The remaining entrance at the front—Nassau Hall's central but modest Georgian doorway and the window above—was enlarged to become the present ceremonial one-and-a-half-story arched Florentine entry. Notman emphasized the symbolic impact of the doorway as the main entrance to the college by placing at the third story a stone balcony with an arched Palladian window that breaks through the cornice into the central pediment. The sharp eye can see the outline of a red oak leaf, the state tree, carved in relief in the center of the middle of the three stone brackets supporting the balcony. The vertical thrust provided by the greatly enlarged doorway and the piercing of the cornice is continued by a monumental cupola. Even though it straddles the center of the hip roof like an oversized top hat, the cupola does achieve what undoubtedly was Notman's intent, that is, to rise above the canopy of trees and provide an unforgettable point of reference to the heart of the campus.

Inside, the old wooden staircases were replaced by winding redstone steps in the two new towers; partitions were placed across the east and west hallways to prevent students from rolling cannonballs; and the old cross hallways that accommodated the stairs were united with adjacent rooms to create single chambers. The picture gallery on the first floor was enlarged by an addition on the south for use as the library. To increase the light in an era of meager artificial illumination, Notman added a monitor or clerestory, since removed. At that point, the library had scarcely more than 10,000 books and was open only an hour or so each week.

In 1906 Nassau Hall underwent an additional makeover, although this was more in the way of a major adjustment than a complete remodeling. The task fell to Raleigh Gildersleeve, whose work also appears elsewhere on campus. As already noted, the tops of Notman's towers were beheaded. Inside, the library, which Princeton's first professor of geology and geography, Arnold Guyot (1854–1884), had transformed into a Natural History Museum to house his collection of specimens, became the Faculty Room of what was now Princeton University, rather than College. (A memorial to this great professor, who contributed so much to the school's growing prestige, can be found outside at the northeast front of Nassau Hall. It is, appropriately, a glacial boulder.)

In keeping with his ambition to elevate the university's status, and inspired by a deep Anglophilia shared with the influential and moneyed trustees, President Woodrow Wilson (1902–1910, class of 1879) conceived a ceremonial room modeled after the British House of Commons. Gildersleeve transformed the space into a Senate Chamber that was 76 feet long, 36 feet wide, and 30 feet high. The large windows on the east and west walls were divided by free standing columns and the clerestory was removed. A rich cornice runs around the room 20 feet above the floor. The walls are paneled in English oak. The vaulted ceiling is pierced by lunettes over each window. At the south end, there is a raised dais for the President and officers.

Beyond the obvious improvements over time to the heating, cooling, and lighting systems as well as the welcome addition of plumbing, the building that emerged after Notman's redesign and Gildersleeve's fine-tuning is today's Nassau Hall—with one major alteration, Memorial Hall, which was dedicated on Alumni Day, February 21, 1920. The First World War had a sobering impact on the campus and the entire community. The bronze stars affixed to the walls and window sills of the older dormitories memorialize students and alumni who had lived in those rooms and were killed in the war. The great monument at the head of Nassau Street commemorating the Battle of Princeton also comes from this period of heightened patriotism. The university was moved to make a gesture similarly grand and yet, like the simple bronze stars, intimate. The administration and trustees decided on a solemnly grand statement that would literally come from the historic heart of the University—Nassau Hall.

The Philadelphia firm of Day and Klauder, who as we will discover play a central role in Princeton's architectural history, was commissioned to redesign the large entrance room one walks into after passing through Notman's ceremonial door. What emerges is not the Collegiate Gothic style, for which the firm is best known, but a dignified and resolutely Beaux-Arts space. High, quiet, and spare, the room gives off the air of a chapel. The marble panels inset into the bays between the marble pilasters that process around the room bear the names of those who died in America's wars from the Revolution to Vietnam. Carved into the wall next to the adjoining Faculty Room is the inscription, "*Memoria Aeterna Retinet Alma Mater Filios Pro Patria Animas Ponentes*" ["Alma Mater keeps in eternal memory her sons who laid down their lives for their country"]. The panel commemorating those who died in the Civil War is of particular interest. In a remarkable instance of life imitating art, the number of men who died on the opposing sides is precisely equal, nor is there any indication here of which side they fought on. The fratricidal nature of a conflict that pitted brother against brother, friend against friend, is powerfully underscored by silence. If Notman's redesign of Nassau Hall marked the exuberant beginning of Princeton's Victorian campus, Memorial Hall represents a somber end.

A few words about the tigers: on either side of the low pedestals flanking the front entrance sit a pair of bronze tigers gazing past the FitzRandoph Gates out to Nassau Street. Originally, a pair of lions had occupied this privileged perch. Gifts of the Class of 1879, they had been designed by the distinguished sculptor of the Statue of Liberty, Frederick-Auguste Bartholdi (1834–1904). The lineage of the lions goes back to the rampant feline at the center of the House of Nassau's coat of arms. However, by the end of the nineteenth century, tigers had come to be identified as the school's mascot, while rival Columbia had adopted the lion. Bowing to the inevitable, the Class of '79 banished the lions to another site on campus and in 1911 donated the bronze tigers by A. P. Proctor, their backs since burnished by generations of children.

Along with the lions, the undergraduates have likewise been banished as residents. In 1878 the trustees voted that students would no longer be housed in Nassau Hall. However, it was not until 1903 that the last residents moved out from what was then and sometimes to this day is called Old North.

10. Alexander Hall   *William A. Potter, 1892*

Alexander Hall

After Nassau Hall, the next building is the marvelous Richardsonian Romanesque confection that is Alexander Hall, which honors three generations of Alexander men who served as Princeton trustees. Walking due west from Nassau Hall through the open space that until the 1960s had been occupied by Reunion Hall, one approaches the rusticated brown-

Alexander Hall, auditorium

stone and red granite walls and turrets of a horseshoe-shaped structure that seems to be half church, half nineteenth-century city hall. Alexander Hall was built as a 1,500-seat assembly hall to accommodate large meetings of students and faculty, such as the annual commencement. Its size is a measure of Princeton's accelerating growth in the closing years of the nineteenth century.

In a profession in which achievement and recognition do not often come until middle age, William Appleton Potter (1842–1909) was much the *wunderkind*. A major force in creating the architectural heritage of both the college and the nearby Princeton Theological Seminary, Potter landed his first commission on the Princeton campus when he was still a teenager. He was the son of Bishop Alonzo Potter and a half-brother of Edward Tuckerman Potter, also an architect, and grew up in Philadelphia. The fact that he learned his art in college rather than on construction sites distinguished him from most of the architects of the first half of the nineteenth century, who received their training through apprenticeships in the building trades. Potter's genius did not reside in originality, but in the skill with which he incorporated the ideas of others. For example, the great round Romanesque arches that lead into cavernous doorways are a giveaway that Alexander Hall was inspired by the work of the great nineteenth-century American architect Henry Hobson Richardson (1838–1886). Other Richardsonian features are the steep gabled roof, tall dormers, heavy and rough stone walls, the horizontal emphasis, and the zig zag detail under the eaves.

The orientation of Alexander Hall reveals an important defining characteristic of Princeton's Victorian campus: it faces out to Nassau Street. The new academic and classroom facilities that were built during McCosh's tenure and the years immediately following lined up along Nassau Street. Yes, the neoclassic First Presbyterian Church stands in front between Alexander Hall and Nassau Street, but through no fault of Potter's—he tried to persuade the trustees to tear it down. Succeeding changes to the university's masterplan along with the disappearance of key buildings have tended to obscure this arrangement, while old photographs reveal the complementary relationship with the buildings on the north side of Nassau Street. The university, in other words, had a streetscape with Alexander Hall, Maclean House, Nassau Hall, Chancellor Green Library, Dickinson Hall (destroyed by fire, 1920), and the John C. Green School of Science (destroyed by fire,

1928), all joining with Nassau Chapel and the old University Hall (torn down, 1906) on the northwest corner of the campus to look out into the community. The dormitories and other student facilities were sited to the south, deep into the campus behind this public "wall." The Victorian arrangement of Princeton's private and public faces makes perfect sense and gives the lie to the criticism leveled by the generation of planners and architects who immediately followed that the Victorian campus had no rational plan.

As the university turned inward and away from Nassau Street, the back or south side of Alexander Hall assumed a new importance in the overall campus plan. Today the massive southern elevation with its great Tiffany quatrefoil window helps define the northern edge of a loosely organized quadrangle. Particularly noteworthy is the exuberant exterior *bas relief* sculpture, designed by J. A. Bolger and executed by J. Massey Rhind, which embraces the sides of the great window and supports it from below. The sculpture depicts the arts and sciences paying tribute to *Learning*, the central seated figure, who holds a large book between his left hand and knee. On his left stand figures representing oratory, theology, law, history, philosophy, and ethics; to his right stand architecture, sculpture, painting, poetry, music, and belles-lettres. The horned figure in the large upper left panel represents Moses; on the upper right side sits Christ. Thus, Princeton's motto—"*vet nov testamentum*" ["the Old and New Testaments"]—is figured in the iconography.

Students are less likely to appreciate the iconography than the fact that Alexander Hall houses a first-class performance space, Richardson Auditorium. The present state of the auditorium dates from a major remodeling carried out in 1984. At that time, the rusticated brownstone ambulatory, which shelters the seven entrances into the auditorium, had glass inserted between the arches. This created a sheltered lobby space. Before the remodeling, the auditorium had pews and a central aisle. The chapel-like air this conveyed was replaced in the remodeling by standard theater seating. Fortunately J. Holzer's splendid mosaics behind the stage on the south wall, which illustrate scenes from Homer's *Iliad*, have been carefully preserved. The remodeling also opened up space in the basement that can be used as rehearsal halls.

Over the years the reputation of Alexander Hall has had precipitous ups and downs. It opened to great acclaim, but very soon became the butt of ridicule. One persistent story has it that Alexander Hall was the revenge of a wealthy alumnus who donated a large sum of money with a major string attached: the funds had to be used to build his failed senior thesis in architecture. On a tour of Princeton, Frank Lloyd Wright is supposed to have said that Alexander Hall was the only interesting work of architecture on campus. No doubt Wright was being characteristically perverse, but he does have a point: the dexterity Potter shows in manipulating forms and the sheer delight he takes in his palette of textures and colors right down to the malachite cross hatching of stained glass in the windows are a treasure. Arguably the high water mark of Princeton's Victorian phase, Alexander Hall was also one of the last facilities built in a style other than the soon-to-be-mandated Collegiate Gothic. Under pressure from the trustees, Potter himself would adopt the ascendant Gothic style before he left Princeton to become United States Supervising Architect.

11. Witherspoon Hall   *R. H. Robertson, 1877*

Witherspoon Hall

Named in honor of Princeton's sixth president and the only clergyman to have signed the Declaration of Independence, the dormitory is today part of Rockefeller College, one of five residential colleges for freshmen and sophomores. Prior to the Civil War, Princeton was the college of choice for many Southern students. After the war, support from the states of the former Confederacy dried up. As a consequence, President McCosh turned his sights to the newly rich northern industrial class. One dimension of his Yankee strategy was to build a dormitory that would lure their sons with the prospect of a good education in luxurious accommodations. The result was Witherspoon Hall.

Although the building seems to have been sited without reference to a larger plan, a second look suggests that once again President McCosh and the school's trustees knew exactly what they were up to. Placed on an elevation overlooking the train station, Witherspoon was the first building on campus that acknowledged the ascendancy of the railroad as an entrance to the community and campus. Five stories high and distinguished by a great tower (removed in the 1940s) on the west side facing the tracks, Witherspoon would have been the first building to be seen as the train approached the campus. In effect, it was both a gateway and an advertisement for an increasingly confident College of New Jersey.

Built to house 140 students in eighty rooms, Witherspoon's amenities were many: water closets on every floor, dumbwaiters, and special rooms and corridors for servants. No expense was spared to create what was widely considered to be the most beautiful dormitory in the world. The skin of the building is as exotic as a rare bird. The ground floor is constructed of dark blocks of stone from Newark. The floors above are of blue-gray Pennsylvania marble set off by bands of the darker stone. Each band of windows is of a different shape, perhaps because the architect saw no reason why one floor should not be distinguished from the next. After all they are different floors.

Victorian architects regarded the roof as the crown of a building and, as befits a crown, they instinctively shot off their most dazzling fireworks here. From the cornice to the peak, Witherspoon's roof plays like the final vigorous movement of a Romantic symphony. Gables and dormers break the roof line. Large, asymmetrical towers rise from the west end, while the southwest corner sports a turret with a conical cap. Nor does the action stop at the ridge line, which seems to fizz with stone ornaments called crockets.

To dwell on the exuberance of Robertson's design risks overlooking its practical attributes. Mention has already been made of McCosh's wish for a dormitory that would be a compelling advertisement for the sons of the well-to-do. However, the architect also dealt effectively with more mundane concerns. For example, the interior plan of the building is far more intimate or residential than the massiveness of Witherspoon's footprint on the landscape might suggest. Intimacy was achieved by breaking down the interior into four distinct buildings, each with a separate entryway. With its high ceilings and elevated siting, Witherspoon Hall was designed to be well ventilated. The manipulation of the building's form also opened up the interior to natural light. Witherspoon was as pleasant as it was grand.

12. Edwards Hall *Edward D. Lindsey, 1880*

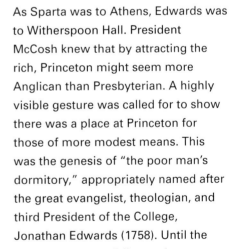

Edwards Hall

As Sparta was to Athens, Edwards was to Witherspoon Hall. President McCosh knew that by attracting the rich, Princeton might seem more Anglican than Presbyterian. A highly visible gesture was called for to show there was a place at Princeton for those of more modest means. This was the genesis of "the poor man's dormitory," appropriately named after the great evangelist, theologian, and third President of the College, Jonathan Edwards (1758). Until the 1960s students paid different rates for dorm rooms, a sliding scale set according to perceived amenities.

Everything about Edwards Hall bespeaks a modest and parsimonious hand. Witherspoon Hall was designed by an architect; Edwards was designed by Princeton's Curator of Buildings and Grounds (1876–1880). Witherspoon had suites and accommodations for servants; Edwards was made up entirely of single rooms. The cost of building Edwards was a third

that of Witherspoon, and not simply because the latter was one story
higher. The materials used to construct Edwards were much more modest—
Trenton brownstone laid randomly and trimmed with a lighter sandstone.
There is no grand porch at the front of the building, which faces east, but
rather a pair of modest arched entrances at the base of Edwards' two
square crenellated towers. Not surprisingly students assigned to Edwards
Hall felt more exiled than accommodated, and the building soon acquired a
reputation for being dark and dirty.

This reputation has been redeemed thanks to an extensive renovation in 1985 by the firm of Fulmer and Wolfe. The roof was raised to create a
fifth floor, the towers were capped with pyramidal roofs, and the gloomy
exterior fire escapes were removed by designing fire safety *into* the dormitory. With these improvements in place, Princeton's upperclassmen suddenly discovered a virtue that was hidden all these years—the single rooms.
For their skillful efforts, the restoration architects earned an Excellence in
Architecture Award from the AIA's New Jersey chapter.

13. Dod Hall *John Lyman Faxon, 1890*

Dod Hall

This upperclass dormitory has been a
thorn in the side of generations of
Princeton's architects and master planners. The criticism focuses on the location, which infringes on the line of
sight leading from Nassau Hall
through Whig–Clio south to the playing fields. Plans to move it have come
to naught. Variously described as
Italianate or Romanesque Revival, Dod
tends to be regarded more highly by the students than by architectural critics. The rooms are, after all, light and airy. When Dod opened, rents for the
one- and two-bedroom suites were between that of Witherspoon and
Edwards; thus students of moderate means favored Dod. The exterior stone
comes from Bull's Island, which is near Trenton. Typical of Princeton buildings, the sills, lintels, and band cornices are limestone. Like Edwards, Dod
opens to the east through three entryways. The central door is flanked by
turrets with conical caps, and framed by a Romanesque arch supported by
two squat pillars of Georgia Creole marble. The interior cast-iron staircases
were an important development in the technology of fire safety. The dormitory is named after Albert B. Dod, a highly regarded Princeton professor of
architecture and math (1830–1845).

Brown Hall

14. Brown Hall   *John Lyman Faxon, 1892*

Brown is the fourth in the series of dormitories (beginning with Witherspoon) that defines a gentle downward sloping diagonal, running from northwest to southeast. In some ways Brown Hall is the most restrained of the parade of Victorian dormitories initiated by President McCosh. Faxon's art may not have been innovative, but it was certainly adroit.

The skill comes in the architect's sure hand in lightening up (figuratively and literally) what might otherwise be a lumpen stone rectangle. The flat jack arches above the windows of the lower two stories, for example, suggest the compression that comes with weight, which is appropriate for the base; the rounded arches of the windows that run along the upper two stories introduce an equally appropriate sense of lightness as well as a vertical note in an otherwise horizontal composition. Or this: the first two floors are built of rusticated blocks of warm gray Cape Ann granite laid in Florentine ashlar style, whereas the top two floors are of orange Pompeian brick trimmed with terra cotta and brick quoins. Again, the eye is drawn up not only by the change in color and materials, but also because the masonry elements themselves are smaller above than they are below. (If the eye roams all the way to the cornice, small terra-cotta lion heads appear at regular intervals. This was at a point in Princeton's history when the tiger had not yet displaced the lion as the school's official mascot.) The corners of the building are further articulated by pairing the windows at the ends of each row, breaking up what might otherwise be a monotonous march of windows across the facade.

In an era of gas lights, introducing natural daylight into the building had to be a high priority. Faxon achieves this in two ways: the windows of Brown Hall are large and generous; the interior court serves as a light well. Prior to air conditioning, the interior court also provided needed ventilation. The architect amplifies the solar wattage by using a more reflective golden yellow brick for the upper stories of the courtyard. Brown Hall is seen at its best advantage, as the architect intended, from the front where the rounded central archway leads your eye to the sunny yellow inside. The way in which brick is used to lighten (in every sense of the word) the overall mass is just one chapter of a building that is a treatise on the art of masonry. Brick buildings of the 1950s and 1960s, which seem to use the material in an absent-minded way, make clear what has been lost. A popular dormitory among the students, Faxon's four-story Florentine palace was nevertheless the last Italianate building built on campus.

15. Prospect House and Gardens and McCosh Walk

Prospect House   *John Notman, 1851; Ellen Wilson, 1904*
McCosh Walk   *1870s*

At the time it was built, Brown Hall enjoyed fine views: the rolling country-side stretched out to the south to the main line of the Pennsylvania Railroad; to the northeast was the floral oasis of Prospect Gardens. The main part of the gardens inscribe a semicircle below the Florentine outline of Prospect, the residence of the school's presidents for a century, from James McCosh in 1868 to Robert Goheen, who moved the official residence off campus to Lowrie House in 1968. The gardens were the special domain of President Wilson's wife, Ellen, when she lived here, 1902–1910.

Reference to the gardens and McCosh Walk highlights yet again how President McCosh transformed almost everything he touched, whether it was students, faculty, architecture, or the land itself. President and Mrs. McCosh had a love for gardening and shaded, parklike walks. Under their influence, the Princeton campus, which prior to the Civil War had been as austere as the architecture, blossomed into a park environment. Princeton hired the school's first landscape architect, Donald Grant Mitchell, who, together with his patrons, set the campus on an enlightened course that persists to this day. No memorial could have been more fitting than to name Princeton's main east-west pedestrian path McCosh Walk after the man who made nat-ural beauty a required subject of the university's spiritual curriculum.

As to Prospect house itself, this fine residence had been donated to the College in 1878 by the pious Stuart brothers, benefactors as well of the Princeton Theological Seminary. The house was originally built for John Potter, the son of a wealthy Charleston merchant. Descended from Scottish stoneworkers, his architect, John Notman, emigrated in 1831 to

Prospect House

Philadelphia, then the center of art and fashion in America. After Prospect house, he would go on to restore Nassau Hall following the fire of 1855. Notman's first major commission was the design of Laurel Hill Cemetery (1836–1839) on a Schuylkill River site. This is the period in the evolution of America's cities when burial of the dead moved from churchyards to romantic outdoor sculpture parks that were the site of Sunday picnics.

Notman specialized in institutional buildings, churches, and villas. His skill was such that he could accommodate whatever currently fashionable revivalist style his clients called for. But he is best remembered for Italianate design, with its mix of classic massing and picturesque composition and ornament. The poetry of Shelley, Byron, and the Brownings, along with the musical compositions of Mendelssohn and Brahms, suggests the depth of the nineteenth-century passion for the Italian Renaissance, a passion that culminated in the art of the Pre-Raphaelites and the influential architectural writings of the great Victorian essayist and critic, John Ruskin. The Italianate was a style especially attractive to newly rich industrialists and tradesmen in Philadelphia—as well as in New York, New Orleans, Cleveland, Chicago, and Detroit—who were moving out of the city to the nearby countryside. Having one's own Tuscan villa instantly communicated the message of "to the manor born." The Italianate was also a style that comfortably straddled the great divide separating the restrained neoclassic, as exemplified at Princeton by Whig and Clio, from the exuberance of the Gothic and Romanesque, as seen in Alexander Hall. As such, it is the aesthetic link that connects the first half and second halves of the nineteenth century. Notman's taste leans more toward the early classicism.

Apart from the prominent off-center tower, the spacious interior is arguably the most noteworthy aspect of the house. Not only do the rooms welcome light and air, they relate to one another in ways that seem to flow easily from how people actually live instead of forcing the residents to follow an abstract geometry in the manner of, say, the symmetrical rectangles of a formal Georgian plan. In other words, far from being arbitrary, the external form is pushed and pulled by what goes on inside. It is organic. This is a major change in residential design that continues to resonate up to the present day.

The central part of the north elevation is the most formal or classic, appropriately so since it is here through the round arches of the *porte cochere* that visitors enter the house. Note how Notman plays with advancing and receding planes, which is characteristic of the Italianate style. Note, too, how he manipulates the number three, from the three rounded arches of the *porte cochere* to the three balustraded balconies, the window lights, and the projecting bays that distinguish this part of the house. The reference to the triangle, that most stable of geometric figures, is probably not an accident: The feeling conveyed is stability and rootedness, which is absolutely appropriate for a great house. Over a century later, I. M. Pei would use the same geometry far more literally for the design of a dormitory, with much the same intent. The most relaxed side of Prospect is at the back, where the dining room, verandah, and conservatory were located. Indeed, the interior plan seems to pull the visitor irresistibly past the formal public rooms at the front to the delightful private spaces at the rear with their view of the garden. Prospect is well-named. The painted steel sculpture, *Moses*, on the front lawn is by the American sculptor, Tony Smith (1912–1980).

Over the years, the interior of Prospect has been subject to the shifting tastes of its various occupants. This has affected everything from window treatments to the colors of the walls. At one point all of the interior was stripped down and painted white, no doubt the result of a resurgent neoclassicist impulse at the beginning of the twentieth century. Changes in technology also reshaped the interior spaces. Lighting fixtures have been changed as the technology of artificial illumination developed. Advances in plumbing and heating, not to mention more sophisticated code standards for fire safety and handicap access, have altered the look of the rooms. For a long time, change was instinctively equated with

Prospect House gardens, rear elevation

improvement, especially when Victorian interior design fell precipitously out of fashion.

This is no longer the case. There is renewed appreciation for the deeply saturated colors, elaborately patterned wallcoverings, and naturally rich materials that characterize the Victorian aesthetic, fueling recent efforts to restore the interior finishes and furnishings to an approximation of what McCosh might have seen when he moved in. The result is a celebration of colors and textures that compels a re-evaluation of Victorians as being dour and strait-laced.

After President Goheen (1957–1972) moved off campus to the Walter Lowrie House, also designed by Notman, Prospect was converted and remodeled into a dining and social center for the faculty. The modern two-story cast-in-place concrete-and-glass dining wing at the southeast corner is skillfully handled. Taking its cue from Notman, it capitalizes on the garden view. While uncompromisingly modern, the addition is still a good tenant, enhancing rather than upstaging.

16. Murray Hall and Dodge Hall

Murray Hall   *H. S. Harvey, 1879*
Dodge Hall   *Parrish and Schroeder, 1900*

Dodge Hall

North and slightly west of Prospect are the pair of linked structures called Murray-Dodge. During the course of its long history, Princeton has witnessed episodes of religious revival. In the 1870s one such surge washed over campus. The focus was the Philadelphia Society, the oldest collegiate religious organization in the country. As the revival gained steam, it soon became obvious the Society needed space in which to meet and pray. Murray Hall was the result, paid for not by the College but students and alumni. The siting of the building was no accident. Murray lines up on the east–west axis defined by Whig–Clio. The grouping indicates a deliberate effort to identify a precinct or zone behind Nassau Hall on the other side of Cannon Green for student extra-curricular activity. Of course, the gleaming temples of Whig–Clio could not have been more different from the large, rusticated brownstone blocks of first Murray and then Dodge Hall. But there is a higher, perhaps unintended logic to the arrangement: the cool, white classic shapes of Whig–Clio served the rational exercise of the intellect; the darker, vaguely ecclesiastical detailing of the Romanesque design of Murray Hall spoke to the irrational yearnings of the soul.

One story in height, Murray Hall, the easternmost of the two structures, is built in a Romanesque style, which characteristically emphasizes the masonry. It is organized as two distinct volumes connected by a vestibule, which serves as a hinge between the two parts. The room to the south was designed to be a large auditorium-cum-prayer hall that seated 400. It is illuminated by a clerestory. The room to the north is a high-ceilinged octagonal reading room. The building honors the memory of a young alumnus, Hamilton Murray, who was lost at sea in 1872.

Having outgrown Murray Hall by the end of the nineteenth century, the Philadelphia Society commissioned architects Parrish and Schroeder to design a two-story building immediately to the west. The new structure, Dodge Hall, was connected to Murray by a 52-foot-long covered walkway, or cloister, pierced by a procession of pointed-arch windows. By contrast to Murray's nineteenth-century Romanesque form (and the dominant style on campus), Dodge rose up in the University's now official twentieth-century style, Collegiate Gothic. Parrish and Schroeder followed several strategies to help make the two distinct buildings seem to be of a piece: they used the same brownstone for Dodge, and over at Murray renovated the roof to look more Gothic. To give the resulting ensemble a focus as well as a presence on campus, the architects designed a 51-foot tower pierced by oriel windows on the northeast corner of Dodge. The Dodge family gave the funds in memory of W. Earl Dodge Jr., Class of 1879.

A century later, the Murray-Dodge complex continues to minister to student social or extra-curricular needs. Dodge is today the headquarters of the University's student religious organizations and houses the offices of the Dean of the Chapel; Murray is the home of Theatre Intime and, downstairs, Princeton's Gay and Lesbian Alliance. At the south and somewhat tucked between the two buildings is another of Princeton's pleasant garden "rooms." In the center is a polished marble tablet given by the class of 1969 on the occasion of their 25th reunion. The inscription, quoting the lyrics of a Joni Mitchell Woodstock song, celebrates the spiritual revival of the bell-bottomed, love bead, counter-culture of the late 1960s and early 1970s. To the north, between Murray-Dodge and East Pyne stands *Two Planes Vertical Horizontal II,* a stainless steel sculpture by American sculptor George Rickey (1907–).

17. East Pyne Hall   *William A. Potter, 1897*

Beyond the Rickey sculpture stands the impressive Tudor Gothic outline of a large structure that began its tenure on campus as Princeton's main library. Formerly Pyne Library, today East Pyne, the building has been extensively remodeled internally to house the classrooms and offices of the University's foreign literature departments. The result is something of a warren of office cubbyholes. East Pyne is a transitional building. It attempts

East Pyne Hall

to bridge the emerging gulf between the fanciful Victorian of the McCosh era and the emerging passion for Collegiate Gothic ushered in by Princeton's Sesquicentennial. The exuberance of the surface detailing together with the heavy rusticated brownstone building material and passion for light are characteristically Victorian. But the attention to symmetry and a strong east-west axis through a closed quadrangle indicate a real shift in course. East Pyne is also Potter's last work for Princeton. Universally admired for his skill as a builder, if not always for his taste, he was soon afterwards appointed United States Supervising Architect.

Once the decision had been made to incorporate the old Chancellor Green Library as the main reading room of a new library complex, Potter had to choose the same brownstone for the sake of harmony. However, the decision to preserve Chancellor Green Library resulted in another, distinctly *un*harmonious consequence. With Chancellor Green on the north, Nassau Hall to the west, and the relatively new Dickinson Hall to the east (destroyed by fire in 1920), the only direction the new library could be sited was to the south. This required razing the school's first free-standing Chapel (1846) along with the well-loved East College dormitory. The destruction of these two buildings—East College in particular—provoked a great outcry from the alumni, who called it the "Crime of '97." A further consequence was to erase the neoclassical symmetry of the Cannon Green quadrangle just as the siting of Chancellor Green had destroyed it to the north, although the architect aligned the west wall of Pyne along the foundation of East College.

Even though Potter was forced by the trustees to design a Gothic quadrangular structure with an eye on Oxford (the trustees had summarily rejected his first five plans), his dexterity was no less inspired here than it was when as a teenager he designed Chancellor Green more than twenty years earlier. Whereas the older building was clearly the work of a young man testing his skills, Pyne Library is the product of a mature sensibility. His main challenge was what to do with a structure that by definition had to be a large warehouse for books. As a major repository for paper-based collections, it had to be fireproof. It also had to be well illuminated inside and, in an era before air conditioning, the library had to be well ventilated.

Potter addressed the need for light and fresh air by opening up the center of the structure and maximizing the use of glass in the walls of the resulting interior court (dedicated to Henry B. Thompson, class of 1877, the influential trustee who selected Princeton's first supervising architect, Ralph Adams Cram). The court provided a steady stream of indirect natural light for the library in an era when the candle power of artificial illumination was limited. A moat around the perimeter admitted light and air into the basement level. Advances in contemporary technology allowed the floors in the stack areas to be paved in thick, translucent glass, thus admitting even more light. Potter's design is also an exercise in state-of-the-art fireproofing. There are no wooden stairways; even the railings are decorative cast iron, a relatively inexpensive manufactured material that could be cast into any shape.

The most distinctive feature of the building is a large tower that rises over the western arch. A shorter, crenellated tower marks the east. As he had at Alexander Hall, Potter again turned to the sculptor John Massey Rhind to decorate the solid planes of the exterior walls. Two of Princeton's greatest Presidents, both of whom were Scottish Presbyterian ministers, occupy opposing monumental niches at the sides of the west archway. John Witherspoon stands at the left with his hands folded, looking out benignly at the university he steered through the Revolutionary War when the campus was literally a battlefield. President James McCosh stands to the right. Above McCosh, niches are occupied by James Madison (class of 1771) and Oliver Ellsworth (class of 1776). The sculptor's fluid handling of the stone, particularly the drapery, is a delight. Additional empty niches on the exterior and within the courtyard suggest that Pyne Library was over time supposed to become a Princeton Valhalla. It would be a splendid tradition to revive. Beneath a sundial placed flush against the south side of the west tower is an inscription: "*Pereunt et Imputantur*" ["they pass away and are charged to our account"].

Since the new library complex would be able to house no fewer than 1,250,000 books, the trustees calculated it would take at least two centuries before all the shelves were filled. The University's calculations were off by 150 years.

18. Chancellor Green Hall (formerly Chancellor Green Library) *William A. Potter, 1873*

The construction of Chancellor Green Library represented one of the first major projects built during President McCosh's tenure. Construction of this vitally needed facility was made possible in no small part as a consequence of a new funding strategy. Until McCosh had come to Princeton, it had been common practice to name a facility after a revered figure (Stanhope and Nassau Halls), its function (Philosophical Hall), or its site (East and West

Chancellor Green Hall

Colleges). It was McCosh who began the lucrative practice of offering to name new facilities after significant donors. In this instance, the library was underwritten by John C. Green (1800–1875), an exceptionally generous trustee, to honor his younger brother, Henry Woodhull Green, the Chancellor of New Jersey's Equity Courts.

The building of the library represented another first—the first major breach in the early nineteenth-century neoclassical quadrangle developed by Latrobe and Joseph Henry. The school's abrupt change in course necessitated tearing down an older structure. Latrobe's Philosophical Hall was razed, not because there was no other land available, but because McCosh wanted Princeton's first free-standing library to occupy a highly visible and symbolically strategic site between Nassau Hall and the then-existing College Chapel. Even more significant, the library faced out toward Nassau Street, rather than internally. This is not easily appreciated today, since Henry House occupies the space between Chancellor Green and Nassau Street. But the change in the orientation of the college is key to an appreciation of how McCosh was reviving the college and in the process reinventing it. The decision to face the library toward Nassau Street was animated by the same spirit that prominently sited Witherspoon looking over the train station. Princeton's new buildings were no longer self-referential in a neoclassical vein, but externally directed to the world beyond the campus. As McCosh was to say in his farewell address, "I viewed edifices as a means to an end."

McCosh's commitment to the future was evident in his efforts to design and build state-of-the-art facilities. The library was the centerpiece of this commitment, since to succeed would signal a revived college intent on achieving world-class status among institutions of higher learning. The college sought advice on every detail from building materials, reading rooms, light, ventilation, heating, to shelving. It took a surprising risk by turning to an unknown design talent for whom the library would be his first major commission: architect William A. Potter, 19 years old.

Perhaps influenced by the precedent of Jefferson's Rotunda at the University of Virginia, Potter played with circular shapes. His concept was to string a series of three octagons along an east–west axis, the central one of which was the dominant structure where most of the books were stored. Each side of the main building was capped by a pediment and pierced by slender windows. At the center of the roof is a stunning stained-glass octagonal skylight. Unlike East Pyne, which was Potter's other library on the Princeton campus, the interior of Chancellor Green remains structurally intact, right down to the gilded iron-work of the perimeter-hugging balcony, which is supported by slender columns topped by capitals of luxurious gilded flowers.

From the outside, the building is a Victorian Gothic fairyland of towers, broken facades, steep roofs set off by varicolored slate, and Romanesque doors and windows. No opportunity for iconographic ornament is overlooked. The polished marble pillars that support the two north entry porticos are topped by limestone capitals, which are carved to resemble stacks of books, their authors' names chiseled into their "spines." Over the center of the main building rises an elliptical cast iron mandala that would appear to symbolize "Christ from Whom and to Whom all knowledge flows."

Chancellor Green, interior

What at first glance might seem to be Victorian fantasy run amuck is in fact a carefully choreographed and innovative response to the user's needs. In an era when artificial illumination left something to be desired (including the danger of fire), admitting an abundance of natural daylighting was essential. This suggests that the complex geometry of the library was not arbitrary, but in fact an imaginative strategy to flood every corner of the interior with light to accommodate scholarly pursuits. To minimize glare, Potter used stained glass in the transoms and most magnificently in a splendid skylight, which has the playful grace of an image from a child's kaleidoscope. The new library was so admired that Princeton awarded Potter an honorary master of arts degree before his 21st birthday.

No longer a functioning library, Chancellor Green Hall has been a candidate for demolition at various times. Fortunately, Princeton has decided that the many delights of this many-faceted Victorian landmark deserve to be preserved for future generations. Currently it serves as the University's Student Center, at least until 2001, when a much larger multipurpose student center opens farther to the south and east on Washington Road, which at the beginning of the twenty-first century is the new geographic heart of the Princeton campus.

Collegiate Gothic

Main Campus

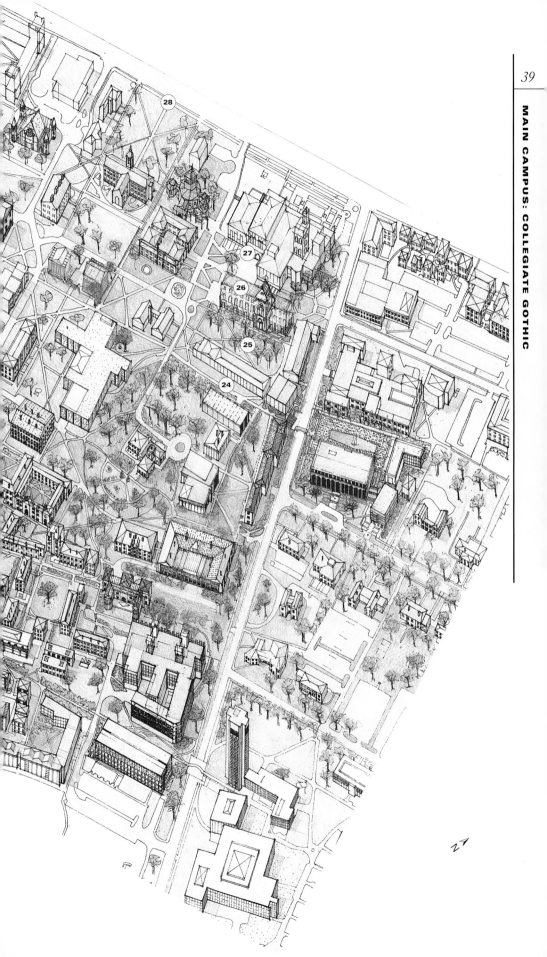

On the eve of the twentieth century, Princeton was well into the process of reinventing itself. Having weathered what was by all accounts a low period in the years leading up to the Civil War, the college had righted itself during the dynamic tenure of McCosh who, along with Witherspoon, was arguably the single most important force in Princeton's history. By the time of its Sesquicentennial in 1896, the college was alive with a new confidence. Adopted by powerful northern industrialists and financiers as patrons, possessing a new physical plant, and having a faculty increasingly distinguished by excellence in teaching and research, Princeton was poised to take its place on the world stage. How better to make a great entrance than to anoint oneself a *University*, throw a big party, and invite distinguished international guests?

Princeton did all this and more. It adopted a style of building meant to identify Princeton as the new standard bearer of a glorious tradition stretching back to medieval Paris and Oxford. The irony is astounding: to achieve the credibility of a great modern university, Princeton looked back in time and dressed itself in Gothic stones.

Collegiate Gothic was mandated by the trustees in 1896. This decision was driven by three men: Moses Taylor Pyne (1856–1921), Andrew Fleming West (1853–1943), and Woodrow Wilson (1856–1924). All had visited England and were struck by the great presence of Oxford and Cambridge Universities—the secluded quadrangles, the separation from the world of action, the sense of higher purpose and community, the apparent spirituality, the dignity of learning, the commitment to educate an elite, and the sheer beauty (right down to the purple chains of wisteria that hung from the walls of ancient stone tracery). And all three were eager to re-create the image if not the spirit of what they had seen.

The transplant was not direct. Instead, the immediate source of inspiration was once again Philadelphia. First at Bryn Mawr and then at the University of Pennsylvania, the young Philadelphia firm of Walter Cope and John Stewardson had designed a series of modern Gothic buildings. The University of Pennsylvania had just moved to a new site and Bryn Mawr had been founded a few years earlier in 1880. For marketing purposes, both schools needed instant credentials, which meant the illusion if not the fact of a distinguished history. This illusion was made more persuasive by deliberately siting the buildings in a irregular way as if the campus had arisen over time.

When Pyne, the rich and influential chairman of the Trustees Committee on Grounds and Buildings (1886–1898), saw that the design vocabulary of Cambridge and Oxford could be spoken so eloquently on his native Mid-Atlantic shores, he put his influence (and money) where his heart was. The trustees forced Princeton's Victorian house architect, William Potter, to design the new library, named after Pyne, as a Tudor Gothic structure. And it was clear to Pyne that Cope and Stewardson would not require similar coaxing. With the construction of Blair Hall (1897, the same year as Pyne Library), Cope and Stewardson and soon after, Day and Klauder, and, most importantly, Ralph Adams Cram (1863–1942) became the new house architects.

Blair Hall, rather than Pyne Library, was the first true embrace of Princeton's long, 50-year love affair with Collegiate Gothic. Professor and later University President Woodrow Wilson enthusiastically endorsed the new face the university was showing to the world. For him Collegiate Gothic was the coming of age for what was now a university, and also an affirmation of Princeton's sacred mission to teach the values and culture of the English-speaking peoples. "Gothic architecture," Wilson wrote in the December 1902 issue of the *Princeton Alumni Weekly*, "has added a thousand years to the history of the university, and has pointed every man's imagination to the earliest traditions of learning in the English-speaking race."

Three points need to be made concerning the trustees' decision to mandate Collegiate Gothic as the official style. First, the decision committed Princeton to a total makeover of the existing campus. To coordinate such a sweeping undertaking, the university created the post of supervising architect, one of the first American universities to do so.

Second, the university was broadcasting a new message. President McCosh had set out in the late nineteenth century to build a contemporary institution of higher learning with German universities as his model. He hired architects who could be counted on to build in the latest Italianate manner. Three decades later, the trustees turned this idea on its head: Germany was out, England in. Collegiate Gothic architecture, as Wilson put it, would turn imaginations back a thousand years "to the earliest traditions of learning." Collegiate Gothic architects like Cram, however, did not consider their work antiquarian. Instead they were simply picking up a tradition that had been interrupted by the Renaissance. Cram and others believed it was possible to resume where the Gothic had left off and go on to even greater achievements. But what they saw as a renewed commitment to a venerable style, their contemporaries were more likely to see as an exercise in nostalgia and instant history.

Third, and perhaps most significantly, the university turned inward, away from Nassau Street. In part this was an inevitable consequence of expansion on newly acquired land to the south. But it was also an expression of a belief that young men needed to sleep, eat, and study away from the distractions of the world. They needed roped off space if they were to bond as a tight, enriching community. The erection of the FitzRandolph Gate between Nassau Street and Nassau Hall (1905) was simply the visible expression of a more rigid separation that now existed between town and gown. Indeed, it was in this period that gates went up around colleges and universities across the land. At Princeton, FitzRandolph Gate would remain shut except on special occasions for nearly seven decades.

19. Holder Hall and Tower

Day Brothers and Klauder, 1910; Venturi, Scott Brown, renovation, 1981

Holder Hall, looking to Campbell Hall and on to Blair Hall

Holder Tower, Rockefeller College

Walk Three on the Main Campus begins to the west of Nassau Hall at the Gothic arch that leads into Holder Court. Commenting on this Collegiate Gothic ensemble, with its picturesque quadrangles and shaded cloisters, Cram said: "In this great group of collegiate buildings at Princeton—Holder Hall and the University Dining Halls—Messrs. Day and Klauder reach the highest point thus far in their authoritative interpretation of Gothic as a living style."

The importance of this remarkable ensemble cannot be overstated. For one, the 140-foot Holder Memorial Tower, modeled after Canterbury Cathedral, fixed in the minds of students and visitors alike an indelible image of Princeton as an old and venerable campus steeped in tradition. On a more practical level, the complex brilliantly addressed two of the most pressing issues faced by the growing university—where would the increasing number of students eat and sleep? The university realized this was a major problem. President Wilson believed that if students had no other social options apart from the Prospect Avenue Eating Clubs, and if there was no place to sleep at the end of the day apart from off-campus housing, it would be next-to-impossible to achieve the ideal *community* of scholars. How else could an attitude of "service to the nation," Wilson's great phrase, be nurtured unless the undergraduates were shut off from the distractions of the so-called Gilded Age? This is the context in which to understand what drove the great burst of dormitory construction in the first decades of the twentieth century as well as various star-crossed attempts to eliminate the Eating Clubs (Walk Five).

The building of the complex that ultimately included Holder, Mestres, Madison, and Hamilton Halls began with Holder in 1909 and continued into the First World War with the completion of Madison Hall. Whereas Cram's praise for Day and Klauder addressed more scholarly matters in their "authoritative interpretation" of the Gothic style, succeeding generations have focused on the beauty of the work. Some might quarrel with the elitist, inward-looking design, but that was precisely what the university asked the architects to do. Also, it is impossible not to marvel at the skill that handled the limestone tracery of the cloister on the west side of Holder Court as if it were plastic rather than stone.

The arch at the center of the cloister leads to Hamilton Court. The contrast between the two courts—Holder to the east and Hamilton to the west—epitomizes the architects' shrewd understanding of how to manipulate our emotional response. Holder Court invites crowds and communal undertakings. It is a spacious parade ground onto which the residents of the various entries that ring the court empty. On the other side of the arch, Hamilton Court is intimate, landscaped, romantic, and quiet. It is a green chapel. (The bronze figure toward the northwest corner of the courtyard, *The Bride*, is by twentieth-century British sculptor Reg Butler (1913–1981).) Day and Klauder's outdoor rooms and architectural masses are original inventions built by imported stonemasons working with up-to-date concrete and steel construction techniques. Their achievement recalls the German poet Schiller's description of architecture as "frozen music."

The great arch on the east side of Holder Court has special significance: as the foundation for Holder Hall was being dug, workmen discovered the remains of a burial ground belonging to the FitzRandolphs, the family that had donated the original four-and-a-half acres for the Princeton campus. President Wilson had the contents of each grave placed in a separate box and reinterred under the arch. A commemorative plaque on the south wall has inscriptions by Wilson and Andrew Fleming West, the first dean of Princeton's new Graduate School. Arguably the more poetic of the two, West's Latin inscription translates: "In our ground he sleeps, nay, rather, in his own."

In 1981 Philadelphia architects Venturi Scott Brown renovated and remodeled the entire complex to accommodate two of the university's new residential colleges, Mathey and Rockefeller. They transformed the five connected dining halls of Madison Hall, known collectively as the "Commons," into dining facilities and common rooms that now serve both colleges. Holder Hall and Tower serve as the residence of Rockefeller College, which also includes Madison, Witherspoon, and part of Blair Hall.

20. Hamilton Hall

Day Brothers, 1911; Venturi, Scott Brown, renovation, 1981

Although Hamilton was regarded initially as a continuation of the U-shaped Holder Hall, it today stands quite well on its own. One of the smallest Gothic dormitories, it is widely admired as one of the most beautiful. Unlike Holder Hall, which is viewed straight on through either the east or west arches, Hamilton is always seen at an oblique angle. Also, the architects force one to slow down when entering this cool precinct of flowering shrubs and deep shadows. Entrance from the east is gained by stepping down a flight of stairs; from the west, by climbing a narrow flight of stairs from University Place. This is a privileged and restorative place. A gift of the classes of 1884 and 1885, it is named for John Hamilton, the acting Governor of the Province of New Jersey, who granted the first charter to the College of New Jersey in 1746. It is one of the residential dormitories of Mathey College, and houses the Laurance S. Rockefeller '32 Library, which is shared with the residents of Rockefeller College.

21. Joline Hall   *Charles Z. Klauder, 1932*

As far back as President Wilson, there was a commitment to complete the university's western-most quadrangle by joining Campbell Hall (1909) to the east and Blair Hall (1897) to the south. This was not possible until Halsted Observatory, which stood in the way, was torn down in 1930. However, by then the Great Depression was beginning to be felt. Perhaps because of the long, narrow site, a diminishing enthusiasm for Gothic architecture, or the increasing financial straits affecting the entire country, Joline feels different.

There is little of the imagination or invention that animates Holder and Hamilton Halls. Instead, Joline is much more sober, even streamlined. Whatever the constraints that shaped it, after Joline was built, it was the last time Princeton broke ground for a new residential dormitory for over fifteen years. Today Joline Hall is one of the residential dormitories of Mathey College. The dormitory takes its name from Adrian Joline, class of 1870.

Joline Hall

22. Blair Hall   *Walter Cope and John Stewardson, 1897*

For all the echoes of Oxford and Cambridge, Blair Hall owes more to Main Line Philadelphia than to the Tudor gate towers of England's oldest universities. The design of Blair Hall, right down to the distinctive crenellated tower with its four corner turrets, is derived from an earlier Cope and Stewardson building, Rockefeller Hall at Bryn Mawr. If it is more dramatic than its Main Line predecessor, the impact has to do with its elevated siting on the slight hill that overlooks the train station. Visitors who arrive at Princeton by train , enter upon a great first act to the rest of the undergraduate campus. The university asked Cope and Stewardson to address a triple challenge: provide space for the growing student population, screen the campus from the noise and pollution of the nearby train line, and give Princeton a new ceremonial entrance that responded to the fact that in the closing years of the nineteenth century, most students and visitors arrived at Princeton by train. The architects delivered on all three counts—and more. Cope and Stewardson's achievement seemed to be visual proof of the wisdom of the trustees' decision to adopt Collegiate Gothic as the official style. Together with Nassau Hall (1756) and Wu Hall (1983), Blair became one of the three most influential buildings on campus.

It provided much needed dormitory space, and the imposing stone walls closed the campus off from the outside world of belching steam locomotives. The function of the building as a line of demarcation or screen is underscored by the fact that all the entryways open to the north onto to the expansive green lawn loosely defined by Witherspoon, West College, Joline, and Alexander Halls. Approached from below by a steep flight of stone stairs, Blair Hall has an imposing, fortress-like air. The arch at the foot of the

Blair Hall, left; *Witherspoon Hall,* center; *Stafford Little Hall,* right

central clock tower would seem to communicate with totally different worlds—those who study above in the quiet, tree-shaded quadrangles and those who work below in the soot and grime. Had the architects placed St. Michael at the top of the stairs with a drawn sword, the distinction between the fallen of this world and the Elect of Eden could not have been more clear.

Blair's function as a screen and as the university's main gateway has been considerably diminished by the relocation of the train station to the south. Nevertheless, Blair Hall retains much of its power, as anyone who walks the long landscaped path from the train station to the foot of the stairs discovers. A distant presence that grows larger and larger with each step, Blair is as much a symbol of the Princeton campus as it is a building that captures the genius of the place. The dormitory is named for the wealthy railroad entrepreneur, John Insley Blair, who donated it.

23. Stafford Little Hall

Cope and Stewardson, 1899 north section and 1902 south addition

In their second project for the university, Cope and Stewardson extended the Gothic western wall begun with Blair. Named for the alumnus (class of 1844) who donated it, Stafford Little follows the property line of the campus as it existed before the train station and tracks were moved south. This explains the dormitory's curious zigzag shape or what Princeton alumnus F. Scott Fitzgerald called the "black Gothic snake of Little." While descriptive of the shape, the words "Gothic snake" do not prepare you for the many delights of this dormitory, including the fact that it was the first to have baths. Where Blair is formidable, Stafford Little has a charm that is

Stafford Little Hall

partially explained by the fact that it does not have to bear the weight of being a grand ceremonial entrance to the campus. The graceful bays of Stafford Little, the Flemish gables, the Tudor chimney stacks, the pedimented doors, and the broad smile of the oriel window in the four-story crenellated tower are the grace notes of a charming composition. But are all the seeming extras really necessary? This prompts another question repeatedly raised by the architecture on Princeton's campus: what is the role of ornament?

Let's for a moment redesign Stafford Little with an eye toward editing out the details that do not keep the students warm and dry. First, replace all the doors and windows with uniform off-the-shelf substitutes sold by any modern home improvement store. Instead of projecting bays, receding planes, and the tower, straighten out and flatten the walls and the roofline. Instead of limestone quoins and window trim, stick to one building material. What remains is a building that still accommodates the same number of students but is now little more than a long wall penetrated at regular intervals by windows and doors. Functional, yes; delightful, no.

24. McCosh Hall   *Raleigh C. Gildersleeve, 1907*

Impressive in size even today, McCosh Hall was built big to accommodate a big idea—President Woodrow Wilson's revolutionary preceptorial system of instruction. The university chose Collegiate Gothic for what was to become Princeton's largest classroom and office complex among a competition among seven architects. It selected the German-trained Gildersleeve to design an L-shaped building 400 feet long on the leg that runs parallel to

Mather Sundial and McCosh Hall

McCosh Wall and 100 feet on the northern extension that fronts Washington Road. Gildersleeve's academic background may have been less an argument for his selection than the fact that he was the clear favorite of Moses Pyne. He had designed two dormitories for the influential trustee on the north side of Nassau Street, which featured retail outlets on the ground floor. In addition, he had remodeled Pyne's great estate on the west side of town, Drumthwacket, which today serves as the official residence of New Jersey's Governor.

Winning the competition and Pyne's powerful support did not mean clear sailing for the architect. The trustees involved themselves intimately in the design process, causing Gildersleeve to modify his concept in a number of ways. As an example, the tower as shown in his winning proposal was in fact ultimately moved back to the northeast corner of Washington Road. Further, the grotesques or gargoyles favored by the architect were erased from the flying buttresses, which at the time were a new design element on campus. Also, the window lintels on the first floor were altered from curved to straight. But the broad outlines of Gildersleeve's proposal remained, including the choice of limestone as exterior cladding with a brick backing as an extra measure of fire protection.

The interior features a large lecture room (known today as the Harold Helm Auditorium) that accommodates 600, two smaller lecture rooms that hold 250 each, and one in which 150 can sit. In addition to faculty office space, there were fourteen recitation rooms and nine separate entrances from campus to minimize crowding when classes change. All the interior wood is oak. Although impressive in size, especially when first built, every inch of new space was needed to house President Wilson's ambitious educational program, which required a great increase in the size of the faculty. However, accommodating Wilson had unforeseen and explosive consequences that will come up in Walk Eight, Princeton's Graduate College.

25. Mather Sundial *1907*

Given to Princeton University in 1907, the Mather Sundial is a replica of the Turnball Sundial erected in 1551 at Corpus Christi College, Oxford. The emotional affiliation President Wilson, Dean West, and Moses Pyne had with the great universities of England is made manifest by one of the oldest pieces of free-standing sculpture on campus. Sir William Mather, MP, governor of Victoria university in Manchester, England, presented the sundial to the university. Surmounted by a limestone self-wounding pelican—an ancient symbol for the sacrifice of Christ—the sundial was for years held in high esteem by the undergraduate seniors who alone were privileged to sit at its base. In the current egalitarian climate, seating is first come, first served.

26. University Chapel *Ralph Adams Cram, 1925–1928*

The university's first space dedicated for prayer and worship was located in what today is Nassau Hall's Faculty Room, although the room itself was then not as large. The first free-standing chapel was built on the site where East Pyne Hall now stands. A modest building, its construction nevertheless provoked great controversy when the surprised trustees discovered it followed what they considered to be a Popish cruciform design. It was replaced in 1881 by Marquand Chapel, which was designed in high Victorian splendor by Richard Morris Hunt (1827–1895). Hunt's building was destroyed by fire in 1920 during a house party weekend. The $2.5 million edifice that replaced it, with its High Church air, would no doubt have astonished those earlier trustees who had objected to creeping Popishness. Today's students and visitors are astonished by University Chapel's extraordinary beauty.

The total destruction of Marquand Chapel and the patriotic afterglow of the First World War no doubt provided the climate necessary for a great gesture. But the reach of that gesture was extended by the sense of mission that drove two men: Princeton's supervising architect, Ralph Adams Cram (1906–1929), and its President, John Grier Hibben (1912–1932). For Cram, who was a High Church Episcopalian, the architecture of a university was all about creating "culture and character." For Hibben, the architecture of the new Chapel would be a symbol of "the continuity of the religious tradition of Princeton, which had its origin in the faith and hope of the early founders." The complementary purposes of both men fathered a building of

University Chapel

beauty and holiness that, apart from being one of the world's largest college chapels, is arguably the high water mark of the Collegiate Gothic style that transformed the campus.

The choice of a site on the east side of campus was in part dictated by the location of Marquand Chapel; the new Chapel was to rise phoenix-like from the ashes. There was a second compelling reason for the site: the university's undergraduate center of gravity was moving eastward. At some future date, the Chapel would not be on the edge, but at the literal and symbolic heart of the university community. The actual building of the Chapel represented an amalgam of traditional and modern construction techniques. Although the foundations and footings are in concrete, the upper structure is load-bearing masonry construction (Pennsylvania sandstone and Indiana limestone). In developing his design, Cram took a similarly hybrid approach, turning to a number of sources for inspiration, most notably the chapel at King's College, Cambridge. Although as Sara Bush notes in her commentary, University Chapel is most like an English medieval parish church in form and plan. (Bush also observes that as built, University Chapel owes a great debt to Alexander Hoyle, Cram's primary assistant.)

We first encounter the architect—*literally*—at the west entrance. In 1991 a 96-year-old man named Clifford MacKinnon revealed he had carved his own head along with that of his boss, Cram, as one of a pair of crockets or "grotesques" on either side of the Chapel's entry portal. Cram to the right is easily identifiable by his glasses.

Staying for a moment at the west portal, the tympanum or triangular space immediately above the double set of doors of the main entrance depicts the "majesty of Jesus Christ," as described by St. John in the Book of Revelations. The inscription of the scroll in Christ's lap is translated, "Who is worthy to open the book?" The figures holding books on either side of the seated Christ are the symbols of the four Evangelists: the lion (St. Mark), angel (St. Matthew), eagle (St. John), and ox (St. Luke). Beneath this scene is carved Princeton's coat of arms—an open Bible with the Latin words, "*Vet Nov Testamentum*" ["the Old and New Testaments"], and the university's motto, "*Dei sub numine viget*" ["Under God's power she flourishes"].

On the south facade, built into the angle between the transept and the nave, is the Bright Pulpit, which bears a quotation from John Bright

University Chapel, interior

(1811–1899), English politician and advocate of religious freedom: "An instructed democracy is the surest foundation of government, and education and freedom are the only sources of true greatness and happiness among any people."

The interior of the Chapel is divided into four parts that suggest the outline of a cross. The total length is 270 feet. The elevation is comprised of three sections or stories, beginning with the arcade, then the triforium at the middle, and up to the clerestory. The first room entered is a low-ceilinged hall called the narthex. From here one proceeds to the nave, named after Hibben, which is the largest area of the Chapel. The sensation you experience after moving from the low-ceilinged narthex into the great expanse of the nave demonstrates the power of architecture to choreograph an emotional response. From the pavement to the crown of the vault the distance is 76 feet. In a wonderful instance of swords being hammered into plowshares, the pews are made from army surplus wood first intended for Civil War gun carriages.

Proceeding down the center aisle, you come to the widest section of the nave, that is, the crossing, where the perpendicular or long arm of the cross intersects the short or horizontal arm. Attached on either end of the crossing are two transepts: Marquand to the left and Braman on the right. Marquand Chapel is used for smaller daily services. The bronze cross is the work of Stephen Zorochin, a campus security guard. The bronze sculpture of James McCosh is a copy using the artist's mold of the original lost in the burning of the earlier chapel made by nineteenth-century Irish-American sculptor, Augustus St. Gaudens (1854–1913).

At the very end of the nave is the chancel, which is reached by a low set of steps. To the left of the stairs is a mid-sixteenth-century pulpit brought over from France; to the right is the lectern. The eagle standing over the snake represents Christ's victory over evil. The chancel is paneled in oak carved in England from Sherwood Forest trees. This one task alone required a hundred woodcarvers who worked on this project for over a year. The oak statues on the ends of the choir and clergy stalls represent musicians, scholars, and teachers of the church. With seating for nearly 2000, the Chapel offers not only religious services, but also theater, dance, and musical performances. Known for its outstanding baroque quality, the Chapel organ has 125 stops and 10,000 pipes. At the rear, in the triforium on

University Chapel

the north wall of the nave is an antiphonal organ. In the west gallery, below the window is a fanfare trumpet for ceremonial occasions.

The intricate stained-glass windows throughout the Chapel memorialize figures from Princeton's history as well as depict scenes from the Bible, literature, history, and philosophy. Of these, the most important iconographically as well as visually are the four Great Windows at the building's four extremes, each depicting a central Christian theme: north—Endurance; east—Love; south—Truth; west—Life. At the center of each window is the figure of Christ depicted, respectively, as martyr, lover (the central scene is the Last Supper), teacher, and savior (the scene is the Second Coming).

A separate book could be written on all the stories told by the richly leaded stained glass that pierces the massive Chapel and makes the walls appear light—in both senses of the word. A few personal highlights: John Witherspoon, the sixth president of the college, is depicted in the Great South Window ("Christ the Teacher"). He stands in the right lancet, beside the medieval scholar Alcuin, and above the seven liberal arts—arithmetic, geometry, astronomy, rhetoric, dialectic, grammar, and music, which constituted the curriculum at the time the great cathedrals were built. In the wall below is this verse from the Gospel of St. John: "Ye shall know the truth, and the truth shall make you free."

In the center of the chancel wall is the Great East Window ("The Love of Christ"). The chancel is flanked by six bays of windows, the first two representing Psalms of David, and the remaining four depicting cycles from four great Christian epics—Dante's *Divine Comedy*, Malory's *The Death of Arthur*, Milton's *Paradise Lost*, and Bunyan's *Pilgrim's Progress*.

Outside, the grounds in the immediate vicinity of the Chapel reveal their own special pleasures. Against the north transept is a small formal garden designed by landscape architect H. Russell Butler Jr. The garden of evergreens and white azaleas is a suitably modest and reflective memorial to John Grier Hibben, the driving force behind the construction of the great Chapel. The nearby bronze sculpture of *Abraham and Isaac: In Memory of May 4th, 1970* is by American sculptor George Segal (1924–). Commissioned in 1979, it commemorates the shooting deaths of four students at Kent State University by National Guard Troops. A happier memory is discovered in a gracefully curved bench next to the Chapel at the northwest corner. It memorializes Princeton's first consulting landscape architect,

Abraham and Isaac: In Memory of
May 4th, 1970, *George Segal*

Beatrix Farrand (1872–1959), whose living monument is the natural beauty that distinguishes the Princeton campus. The inscription reads: "Her love of beauty and order is everywhere visible in what she planted for our delight."

At the rear of the Chapel, connecting the apse with Dickinson Hall, is Rothschild Arch (1930), which memorializes members of the Rothschild family. The relative modesty of the pair of side-by-side limestone arches belies the role this memorial played in slamming shut one of the most significant chapter's in Princeton's architectural history. Outraged by what he considered a desecration of his design, Cram resigned after 22 years as Supervising Architect when he could not convince the university to abandon its intention to build the arch. At the front, in the plaza between the Chapel and Firestone Library is *Song of the Vowels* (1931–32, cast in 1969), a bronze by the American-Lithuanian-born sculptor Jacques Lipchitz (1891–1973).

The site of individual and collective celebration, thanksgiving, grief, and debate, the University Chapel has touched the pulse, and often the heart, of Princeton and the community it serves.

27. Firestone Library and Dulles Library of Diplomatic History

Firestone Library

> *R. B. O'Connor '20 and W. H. Kilham, 1948; O'Connor and Kilham, stack expansion, 1970; Koetter/Kim and Associates, expansion, 1988*

Dulles Library of Diplomatic History   *O'Connor and Kilham, 1962*

The heart of a great university is its library. In the expansiveness of this heart, Princeton is second to no university in the country. With its satellite repositories around campus that together house nearly eight million volumes, Firestone Library represents a studied attempt to resolve a fundamental paradox: books need to be protected, but unless they are accessible they have no value.

For colonial Americans, a gift of books was valued as much as a gift of money, perhaps even more so. The wisdom contained within a book is beyond time and the vicissitudes of human circumstance—but the books themselves

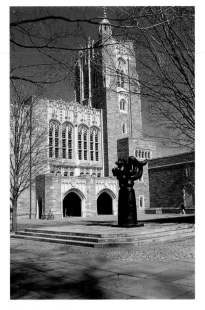

Firestone Library

are not. Initially housed in Nassau Hall, precious volumes repeatedly fell victim to the great fires that reduced the structure to its massive exterior walls. Fire was not the only threat; there was also policy. Because they were precious, books were kept under lock and key except for one hour a week, when students were allowed limited access.

There was also the issue of space. Unlike the considerably younger Princeton Theological Seminary, which had built a free-standing facility as early as 1843, the college even after the Civil War was forced to store its books in whatever space was available. The lack of a separate library facility and the meager size of the collection appalled newly-appointed President James McCosh when he arrived from Scotland in 1868. The library at that point consisted of no more than 14,000 volumes. The two student debating societies, Whig and Clio, alleviated the problem somewhat by offering their own libraries. But a library for "members only" could never replace the need for a college facility that served the needs of the entire student body as well as the faculty.

McCosh's attention to this challenge soon bore fruit. His commitment to growth and, most importantly, *access*, transformed what had been an anemic accessions policy into a rapidly rising tide of new books. At the same time, McCosh liberalized the school's lending policy and the hours during which books could be accessed. His initiatives were met by an explosion of student use; it was impossible to rein it in. First Chancellor Green Library and then Pyne Library, both of which had been intended for the use of many generations, were overwhelmed. By the end of the 1920s, it was clear a larger facility had to be built. Charles Klauder produced sketches in the early 1930s that show a Collegiate Gothic structure with a monumental, if not theatrical, Gothic interior. Klauder's conception focused on a vertical storage of books that, had it been built, would have yielded a structure along the lines of the soaring Cathedral of Learning he had designed for the University of Pittsburgh.

In 1944 President Harold Dodds (1933–1957) convened a star task force of college librarians, library consultants, and a new set of young architects, Robert B. O'Connor and Walter H. Kilham, whose firm had been founded in New York the year before. Called the Cooperative Committee on Library Building Plans, this task force was charged not only to develop a plan to meet the needs of faculty and students, but to scrap all previous

Firestone Library expansion

conceptions and create a revolutionary prototype for what a modern library should be. It was to be a "laboratory-workshop library," not a storehouse where students had to request books at a main circulation desk. To protect books from ultraviolet rays, the stacks would be located underground. Henry Firestone Library was the architects' response.

Commentators have tended to dismiss the design as the last timid gasp of the Collegiate Gothic style. (In fact, it is not. That honor belongs to 1915 Hall, dedicated a year later.) However, the focus should be where the task force placed it, on the inside. It is here that the architects show their real skill. By employing what was then a fairly revolutionary use of a flexible modular system of organization, the architects and their consultants imaginatively tackled the twin challenges of storage and access. In the process they were able to create the world's largest collegiate open stack library.

The grade of the site, sloping down toward Nassau Street, allowed for a large facility that would not overshadow the nearby Chapel. One enters from the south into what appears to be the ground floor of a relatively modest building, but is in fact the third level of a six-story structure. The three floors above and the entrance tower are constructed of reinforced steel clad in rustic buff limestone, Wissahickon schist, and Mount Airy granite to complement Cram's Chapel and McCosh Hall in the near distance. The three floors below grade are constructed of reinforced concrete.

The light-filled two-storied room, immediately to the left of the entrance, is a contemporary update of the great reading halls of earlier libraries such as the Library of Congress. (The lobby contains *White Sun*, a 1966 sculpture by Isamu Noguchi (1904–1988).) The exhibitions room to the right houses a permanent exhibit of the surviving books from the eighteenth-century collection of the College of New Jersey's library. The sight of that tiny collection in the context of the enormous contemporary repository of books that surrounds it reveals at a glance the knowledge explosion that has transformed the very idea of a university. Further inside, elevators and stairs lead to a series of lower levels where miles of open stacks house the library's collection. The stacks themselves are honeycombed with study carrels and reading areas. The great virtue of this modular plan was to offer a flexibility that could easily accommodate what everyone recognized was the inevitability of change and growth.

Understanding that a modern library must always be a work in progress—clearly demonstrated by the rapid obsolescence of Princeton's earlier facilities—the architects designed a deliberate amorphousness into Firestone's envelope. The entrance, which faces and defers to the Chapel, has an appropriately formal facade that conveys an air of permanence. The other elevations, however, were clearly intended to accommodate lateral additions as the pace of acquisition inevitably grew. In effect, the architects drew a hard line at the front, but a dotted line around the rest of the perimeter that could easily be erased. The first major erasure occurred hardly more than two decades later in 1970 when O'Connor and Kilham were called back to add to the stack areas by expanding the two lower floors. Eighteen years later the firm of Koetter/Kim and Associates was commissioned to add approximately 50,000 square feet of stacks, office spaces, and major reading rooms. The architects accomplished this by pushing the two lower floors even farther north toward Nassau Street.

Whereas the original architects deliberately minimized natural daylight in the stack areas to protect the books from ultra violet rays, Koetter/Kim and Associates welcomed the outside in. Having access to new technologies and materials, the architects designed a carefully organized system of roof penetrations that wash the space with light and allow those inside to have reassuring views out. The three large skylit reading rooms also orient the user in what might otherwise seem like a directionless maze. The largest of these rooms runs along what had been the north outer wall of the existing building with a view out the eastern end to Washington Road. The free use of metal girders, barrel trusses, industrial lighting, the exposed stone wall, and the glass skylight that covers the entire space yield a pleasant space in which to research and write a term paper.

If the inside of the addition employs a wide variety of design strategies to enliven the below-grade space, understatement is the prevailing note outside. As the slope of the site falls away toward Nassau Street, the addition slowly emerges out of the ground, ultimately forming a low wall at its northern edge, penetrated by windows that offer views into the stacks and carrels. The 20-foot wide strip of setback that runs between the length of the wall and Nassau Street is developed as an urban park. Passersby are invited to relax and watch the passing scene outside beneath the two parallel rows of zelcova elms. The textures and colors of the elements that appear above grade are chosen to complement the main building, which rises at some distance in the background. The roof terrace, which is visible from the main building, supports a modest garden that is little more than a formal pattern of grassy spaces. On the lawn between the west side of the library and Nassau Street stands a Corten steel sculpture, *Atmosphere and Environment X* (1969–70), by American artist Louise Nevelson (1900–1988). At the northeast corner, a semicircular stump of a stair tower capped by a sloping glass roof brings daylight into the building. It also anchors this edge of the central campus. But the anchoring seems half hearted. Is it coming or going? Is it a work in progress or a ruin?

The effect is nothing like that created by Holder Hall on the opposite, northwest corner: the Holder complex is a bold architectural statement by a Princeton that is asserting its place on the world stage. At the other end of the twentieth century, the structure that occupies the corner of Nassau Street and Washington Road is a stealth building. Does the Koetter/Kim addition maintain a low profile out of extreme deference to the powerful existing architectural fabric down the street? Or is it unwilling or unable to take a stand? The message seems to be, "If you can't say anything nice, don't say anything at all."

On the other hand, as noted earlier, Firestone Library is a work in progress. The footings of the Koetter/Kim extension have been designed to support additional floors. What we may be seeing is merely the opening chapter of the latest volume in the library's growth. If so, it will be interesting to see what design language the new construction will speak. Almost nowhere else on campus are the risks so great. What would be a mistake is far more obvious than what will succeed.

28. FitzRandolph Gate   *McKim, Mead & White, 1905*

FitzRandolph Gate

The university has three works by one of the most famous architectural firms of the twentieth century, McKim, Mead & White. Interestingly, two of these are elaborate and ceremonial gates. The best known, FitzRandolph Gate, is an appropriate place to conclude a tour of the original campus, since it honors the Princeton family that donated the original four-and-a-half acres upon which the College of New Jersey built its first permanent structures. The bequest of Augustus Van Wickle, a descendant of the FitzRandolph family, the gates employ an iconography that refers to the intertwining histories of College and Nation: the republican eagles that regard one another from the central limestone gateposts represent America; the urns on top of the flanking posts recall the decorative urns on the original central pediment of Nassau Hall. The Class of 1970 further expanded the symbolism of FitzRandoph Gate, it broke the tradition of planting ivy at the base of Nassau Hall and requested instead that the main gate, which since 1905 was opened only on ceremonial occasions, be left open permanently, signifying the university's openness to the world beyond the campus. The gate remains open to this day.

McCosh Walk and the Science Precinct

East Campus

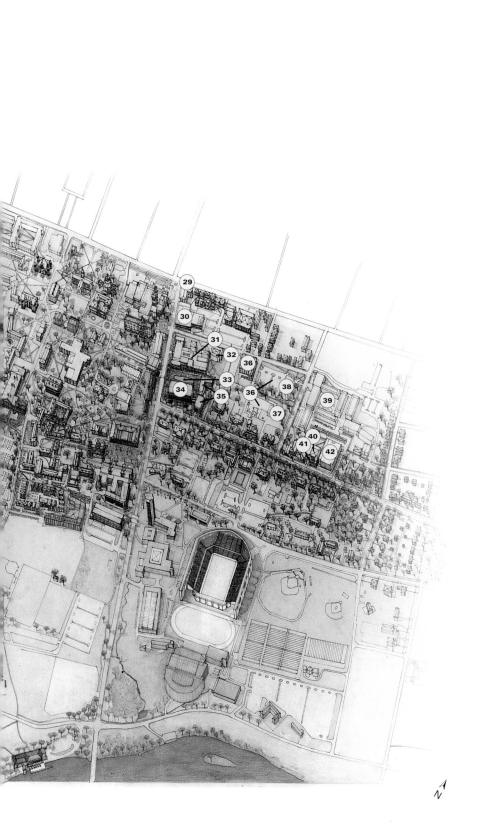

McCosh Walk and the Science Precinct

The Princeton campus east of Washington Road is a work in progress. The newest and most prominent athletic facilities are here, as well as Princeton's storied Eating Clubs. Into this mix sit (somewhat uneasily) two of Princeton's three professional schools—the Engineering School and the Woodrow Wilson School of Public and International Affairs. There are outstanding individual facilities on the East Campus, yet they are scattered among long episodes of architectural mediocrity. With the exception of the Eating Clubs on Prospect Avenue, the buildings in this precinct seldom communicate with one another. Nor does there appear to be an overall plan or design—whether it might be symmetrical, picturesque, or Beaux Arts—which would provide a focus or pull it all together. The east–west axis of McCosh Walk has been extended across Washington Road and runs east to the Engineering Quad. Yet often the Walk seems more like a convenient footpath than a major pedestrian way. And if McCosh Walk begins with a fanfare at Tiger Gate on its western end, it comes to an ignominious conclusion at the eastern terminus by literally slamming into a brick wall. The individual threads of the fabric seem to pull at cross purposes.

There is evidence this is changing. After a generation of aesthetic dithering in the wake of the Collegiate Gothic experience, Princeton's planners have settled on an approach that marries two great traditions. First, there is a renewed commitment to site new buildings with an eye to create rooms and quadrangles, following the example of Cram and his colleagues. At the same time, the university also seems to have returned to an updated Victorian-era eclecticism that embraces a variety of design approaches. A new hybrid or a compromise? Time will tell as newer buildings are added and the total effect becomes more clear.

The Walk takes the reader to and through the various elements that make up the East Campus today, beginning with the Science Precinct north of the Prospect Avenue Eating Clubs.

29. Burr Hall   *Richard Morris Hunt, 1891*

The East Campus walk starts out with a sequence of stylistically unrelated academic buildings at the southeast corner of Nassau Street and Washington Road. Burr Hall is the only surviving example on campus of the work of Richard Morris Hunt, the architect of Marquand Chapel. Perhaps best known for New York's Metropolitan Museum of Art and the Biltmore estate in Asheville, North Carolina, Hunt's architectural style oscillated easily between Beaux Arts pomp and an almost classical, sober use of masonry and massing reminiscent of the American architectural genius, H. H. Richardson. For this science building designed for chemical engineering

Burr Hall

research, Hunt chose a Renaissance Revival vocabulary. The top floors are
of Haverstraw brick laid in red mortar. The ground floor, which flares out
slightly like a skirt, is of Trenton sandstone, as are the belt courses and window trimmings. Mock battlements add visual interest to the straight-for-
ward flat roof.

Burr Hall, solid and serious, was the first academic building east of
Washington Road; it set the pattern for what was to become the university's
scientific precinct. It currently houses the Department of Archeology.

30. Green Hall   *Charles Z. Klauder, 1927; Francis W. Roudebush, remodeling, 1963*

Green Hall and its neighbor Frick Laboratory, is one of the few Collegiate
Gothic buildings built east of the great divide that is Washington Road.
Named for John Cleeve Green, founder of the university's Engineering
School and the donor behind Chancellor Green Library, Green Hall now
houses the Departments of Psychology and Sociology. The Green name or,
more accurately, fortune, is justly associated with this precinct. In the middle
decades of the nineteenth century there was great concern that Princeton
was not responding to the nation's growing need for men trained in the theoretical and applied sciences. It was John Green who decisively stepped up to
the challenge. He endowed chairs, subsidized faculty salaries, and funded the
laboratories and classrooms for the new School of Science. It was Green's
checkbook that provided the resources to turn President McCosh's vision of a
revitalized Princeton into a reality. Behind the distinguished achievement of
the university's departments of chemistry, physics, electrical engineering, and
civil engineering one name is preeminent: John Cleeve Green.

31. Frick Laboratory

Charles Z. Klauder, 1929; O'Connor and Kilham, addition, 1963

Frick Laboratory

The Pittsburgh steelmaker Henry Clay Frick (1849–1919) wanted Princeton to have its own law school. President Hibben had a different agenda and managed to persuade Frick to provide the funds to house the chemistry department in a fine new home. Set in a landscape designed by Beatrix Farrand (the gnarled aged wisteria vines seem to grow out of the stone), the almost residential facade masks a thoroughly modern interior that boasts two of the most extensively used lecture halls on campus. Modest three-story towers on the north and south ends of the two-story western facade and a double-arched entrance are rendered in the mandated Collegiate Gothic style. But there are subtle indications that the business of Frick is more scientific than humanistic. There is no steeply-pitched roof dressed with gables and gargoyles. Rather, the flat line of the roof conveys a certain deliberateness appropriate to the practical scientific investigation going on inside.

Frick Laboratory as well as Green Hall is the leading edge of what Cram as Supervising Architect clearly intended for the emerging campus east of Washington Road. Had this come to pass, the East Campus might have achieved an aesthetic coherence or point of view. But this never happened. Frick and Green were built in the final days of the Roaring Twenties. After the stock market Crash in 1929 and the onslaught of the national Depression, new construction ground to a halt. Before it resumed, Collegiate Gothic had gone out of fashion. The east campus would develop architecturally in a piecemeal fashion.

Although land was available for the future growth of Frick Laboratory, it was not until the 1960s when new technologies, a growing student population, and, most importantly, funds were available to support expansion. Major internal modifications became necessary as a consequence of a fire in 1968. A $1.5 million grant from the Kresge Foundation enabled an additional upgrading of the interior, so that today the only original elements of Klauder's design are the exterior and the auditorium, which was renamed after Sebastian S. Kresge.

Hoyt Laboratory

Toward the end of the 1970s, a decision was made not to expand Frick further, but to construct an entirely new facility for biochemistry that would be oriented toward the north, facing William Street. This is the genesis of the three-story Hoyt Laboratory, which is attached to the older building at the second floor by a skybridge. Taking its cue from the advanced research into the relatively new discipline of biochemistry, the crisp and clean polish of Hoyt "reads" up-to-date. Compare that to Klauder's design for the Frick Laboratory, which is really a Gothic mask that offers few visual clues to the advanced research inside. Whereas Klauder invoked a late medieval academic tradition, Davis Brody and Associates used the new and shiny modern style to communicate a far different message about the university's commitment to innovation and the future.

However, the architects are not above making witty allusions to the past. For example, the passageway underneath the skybridge is a pointed arch. The presence of a tower at the southeast corner is another way of affectionately echoing the older tradition without mimicking it. The stair tower appears to have been neatly sliced from the corner of a rounded square, then pulled partially away like a cut piece being lifted out of a cake. The tower itself is entirely masonry except for a clerestory on top. The effect suggests the beacon of a lighthouse. The architects show an understanding of how to use windows decoratively as well as functionally, which distinguishes this building from the architecture of the 1950s and 1960s where windows are hardly more than utilitarian openings for ventilation and light. The clean edges of the building's geometry evoke Pei's roughly contemporary upperclass Spelman dormitories on the South Campus. This new aesthetic does not hanker after the authority of a medieval past; Hoyt celebrates the possibilities of a more rational, scientific future. Somewhat of an understated reinforced concrete jewel of a building, Hoyt seems to be playing an additional game: Together with Frick on the west and Corwin on the south, Hoyt appears to have taken the first steps necessary toward creating yet another quad. If so, it will no doubt have to be reconfigured, since the main entrance currently looks out to the street.

33. Scudder Plaza and Fountain of Freedom

James Fitzgerald, 1916

Farther down Washington Road, the university makes another attempt to come to terms with modernism without giving up too much of the past. The result is of course a quad, but like no other quad on campus: in one place stand four important chapters in the book of twentieth-century architecture. Here there is the Collegiate Gothic Frick Laboratory on the north, an austere Cold War brick box *cum* cylinder (Corwin, 1952) and a postmodern facility (Fisher Hall) on the east, and a flamboyant recollection of the Parthenon (Robertson Hall) on the south, all standing around a sunken plaza with a pool and fountain (Scudder Plaza and the *Fountain of Freedom* designed by James Fitzgerald). Scudder Plaza with its ample benches, play of waters, and tulip magnolias on the north side mediates among the conflicting messages and somehow calls a restful time out.

34. Robertson Hall *Minoru Yamasaki, 1965*

Robertson Hall

Arguably one of the most memorable if not curious structures on campus, Robertson Hall strikes a defiantly contrary pose. Whereas the austere Cold War or modernist idiom (exemplified by Corwin Hall immediately to the east) speaks in the language of flat unadorned roofs, manufactured brick of relentless sameness, the absence of ornament, and an indifference to the classic three-part hierarchy of base, shaft, and roof, Yamasaki (1912–1986) has designed a building that flouts many of the functional Modernist rules with giddiness. Here is a classical assemblage of pedestal, column, and entablature—all blindingly white in the sunlight. With its signature ribbon of 58 load-bearing quartz-surfaced tapering concrete columns, Robertson Hall tries to bring fun back into modern architecture. Yet if one of the hallmarks of modernism is mechanical repetition, Yamasaki succeeded only in doing a variation on a theme: the arched bays and altogether too skinny columns march in lock step around the perimeter like faceless automatons.

Whatever else might be said about the earlier Collegiate Gothic style, it recognized that growth and change are facts of life. By contrast the very singularity of Yamasaki's design seems to be an attempt to freeze time and forestall future alterations. Prevented by a rigid design from going up or sideways, the university had little choice but to burrow when more space was needed. On the west side under the lawn, a student carrel area was added; also, an entirely new building, Fisher Hall, was built to the southeast and connected to Robertson by an underground pedestrian way.

Thus a significant portion of the building's functioning spaces are hidden from the eye of the pedestrian. Below the first floor is a full level of lecture halls, classrooms, and conference rooms. On the ceremonial first floor are Dodds Auditorium, the library, and a dining hall. Offices are on the top floor behind the grille that wraps around the building in the manner of a monumental, if not top-heavy, cornice. The architect gave Robertson transparency through a liberal use of plate-glass expanses, soaring interior spaces visible from the plaza, and open balconies. This transparency is best appreciated at night when, the building fully lit, light spills out in all directions. The orientation to a plaza, which is part of Yamasaki's overall scheme, makes the point that the building serves the pedestrian not the automobile.

At the time the university dedicated the building, Yamasaki made much of the uniqueness of his design in response, as he said, to the building's special program. Others, however, noted the fingerprints of earlier designs as, for example, the Seattle World's fair and various corporate facilities. A visit inside the building shows Yamasaki's extravagant use of space. All in all, Robertson Hall is a one-act play that had no sequels at Princeton. Even Yamasake's other campus building, Peyton Hall (1966), one block down the hill, is to Robertson what a hangover is to a binge—a sober reflection on the wild party of the night before.

35. Bendheim Hall and Fisher Hall

Venturi, Scott Brown and Associates, 1991

Bendheim and Fisher are of a piece, a modestly handsome piece. Together with the older Corwin and Robertson Halls, to which they are connected, they constitute a large complex that serves the social sciences. The architecture of Bendheim-Fisher announces yet another aesthetic in this stylistically diverse neighborhood, an aesthetic that like Victorian architecture

Bendheim Hall

celebrates color, texture, and light. To see Bendheim and Fisher Halls set at an obtuse angle next to the plain vanilla moderne modernism of Corwin Hall (1952) is to appreciate in an instant what Robert Venturi's polemic,

Complexity and Contradiction in Architecture (perhaps the single most trenchant critique of the relentless Puritanism of modern architecture), had set out to overturn. Both structures are essentially rectangles. Both are brick and glass with limestone trim. But Corwin appears to be the dull shell out of which a far livelier Bendheim (International Studies) and Fisher (Department of Economics) have hatched. Venturi manipulates the geometry of the envelope by rounding the edges and achieves a warmth inside by opening the spaces to sunlight and choosing rich wood finishes.

Robert Venturi and his design partner, Denise Scott Brown, are two names that surface repeatedly in Princeton University's design history after 1980. In turning to this Philadelphia architect and alumnus ('47), Princeton has found in Venturi a designer who has given the school a coherent visual identity second only to that imposed by Ralph Adams Cram. Still the comparison underscores the magnitude of the difference. Whether any other architect will ever have access to the financial resources and the sense of mission necessary to trump Cram and his Collegiate Gothic peers is questionable. Their work—both the individual buildings and the larger plan—is as inescapable as the Alps of Switzerland. All that a contemporary architect can do is acknowledge the achievement and work around it without looking ridiculous. Here, as elsewhere on the Princeton campus, Venturi, Scott Brown manage to do that and often more.

36. Wallace Social Center and Friend Center for Engineering Education

Wallace Social Center *Bohlin Cywinski Jackson, 1999–2000*
Friend Center for Engineering Education
  Henry Cobb, Pei Cobb Fried and Partners, 1999–2000

The main pedestrian route into the academic precinct of the East Campus is McCosh Walk, which has been extended eastward between Corwin Hall (south) and Hoyt Laboratory (north). But the architectural energy that characterizes the immediate vicinity of Washington Road suddenly gives out in a two-block smear of surface parking lots. Literally and figuratively, McCosh Walk loses its edge. However, this is changing. At this writing, the land to the east of Corwin and south of McCosh Walk (behind the former Dial Eating Club) is being excavated for the foundation of Wallace Social Science Center, designed by architects Bohlin Cywinski Jackson.

Wallace will begin to define a new, informal quadrangle that includes Hoyt, Frick, and Corwin. A second quadrangle to the east will take shape thanks to another project currently in the planning stage, the Friend Center for Engineering Education, designed by Henry Cobb of Pei Cobb Fried and Partners. The Friend Center is planned to link up with the northwest edge of the existing Computer Science Building and continue west parallel to William Street. Behind the one-story limestone and glass structure on William Street, a glass box is designed to extend south to and define— along with the Computer Science Building and Mudd Library—the eastern terminus of McCosh Walk. On the other side of this key axis and slightly to the west, Wallace will provide a wall for and welcome definition to McCosh Walk. As an edge building, it is not surprising that the shape of the Bohlin Cywinski Jackson design is rectangular with monumental covered entrances at either end and a one-story triangular glass canopy to shelter pedestrians as they exit McCosh and walk down to a lower level of the building.

The design for Wallace calls for an unmistakably postmodern build-ing, but not with the tongue-in-cheek raid on bits of history for decorative effects, as the term postmodern typically suggests. Here, the architects sub-tly (rather than blatantly) borrow from Princeton's earlier architectural tradi-tions. References to the past are intended to enrich the texture and to impart a recognizable sense of place. Familiar elements include brick and limestone for the building's envelope, which are common to the campus' eastern precinct, broad-eaved roofs that hang over the stair towers (recall-ing Notman's Italianate towers), the classical three-part division of the build-ing's mass, and regular notches in the brick face that mimic Collegiate Gothic crenellation.

But the architects do not want you to think Wallace is an exercise in nostalgia. The brick facing McCosh Walk is a thoroughly modern gesture, hanging as it does like a long billboard on what is the second story of a glass curtain wall. No doubt the single most telling modernist detail is that Wallace is all about straight lines, squares, and rectangles. Given the large surfaces of glass used at the first and third stories as well as the entrances. Wallace should be a transparent lantern that warmly lights up the night along McCosh Walk.

37. Seeley G. Mudd Manuscript Library

Hugh Stubbins and Associates, 1976

Mudd Library on the west side of Olden Street does not share a similar infatuation with transparency and light. Indeed, light can be a dangerous enemy. Built at a cost of $2.5 million, Mudd, which is one of Firestone's eighteen satellite libraries around campus, houses the collected personal papers of public figures, including Adlai Stevenson '22 and Supreme Court Justice John Marshall Harlan '22. The building was named for its benefac-tor, Dr. Seeley G. Mudd, a renowned medical educator and philanthropist.

Given the relative isolation of the site at the time Mudd Library was built, the 31,000-square-foot building did not have to defer to any other structure. Certainly it did not have to relate to the featureless Engineering Quadrangle, its nearest neighbor, on the east side of Olden. Thus, Mudd is a stand-alone act, a reinforced concrete frame wrapped in liver-colored brick. Although the architects did not have to defer to other facilities in their design, they did have to accommodate specific demands of the building program: sunlight and paper-based artifacts, for example, were incompatible. The architects thus limited the placement of windows to public and staff areas. The stacks are entirely enclosed and access is strictly controlled. Other defensive strategies are built into a storage facility for irreplaceable documents: sophisticated climate control and a fire protection system using non-toxic halon gas, not carbon dioxide, to extinguish fire. Mudd was also the first building on the Princeton campus designed to comply with the university's new energy conservation program initiated in response to the Arab Oil Embargo of the 1970s.

The orientation of the building to the north, facing McCosh Walk, and the overhang created by the vault reduce sun radiation, allowing for a relatively large expanse of glazing that runs around the perimeter. The irregular color and shape of the hand-crafted bricks create an engaging texture that is quite different from the relentlessly smooth manufactured brick of the Engineering Quadrangle across the way. Although the effect is subtle, this texture allows the brick to reflect ambient light. An essentially background modernist building, Mudd does the job well with a high level of craftsmanship that is not without its simple pleasures.

38. Computer Science Building

Kliment and Halsband Architects, 1989

Computer Science Building

Home to Princeton's department of computer science, the 57,000-square-foot building includes classrooms and a lecture hall on the ground floor and basement level; student, faculty, administrative offices, seminar rooms, and research laboratories are housed in the upper three stories. Sited on the northern edge of McCosh Walk as it reaches toward Olden Street, the Computer Science Building gives a welcome focus to this important east–west pedestrian way and begins to define, in the words of its architects, "a language for the development of subsequent buildings that will form a new quadrangle."

The building is organized around three entrance towers on the south and west, which visually and functionally anchor the structure. Although the stairtowers do not in fact break the roof line of what is mainly a long brick rectangle, they are clearly announced by entry doors, a bowing out of the dominant rectilinear envelope and a change in the color and nature of the materials that clad the building: The prevailing red brick relaxes into a combination of limestone and brick, in which limestone headers are introduced into the flemish bond. The result is a pleasing houndstooth effect that breaks up what would otherwise be a visually monotonous surface. A limestone colonnade connects the south and west entrances; the south and west elevations open to the outdoors through large glass surfaces, at night sending out a warm glow from inside.

If the limestone trim surrounding the tower windows takes its cues from an older Princeton tradition, so too does the trim of the aluminum windows, which are painted gray to resemble leaded panes. The main stairway is detailed in oak wainscoting and painted steel. This set of stairs links the principal entrance on McCosh Walk with the reception room and tea room on the second floor, which is the facility's chief social space. An additional amenity of the tea room is a balcony that looks out to the west, again in anticipation of what will be the newest of the university's outdoor rooms. A side note: according to the architects, the recessed brick headers visible at the upper left of the west entrance form a conjectural proposition from computer theory in binary code. Not so arresting as a Gothic gargoyle, this whimsical gesture is yet a witty return to ornament and symbolism.

What is most outstanding about the design is in fact invisible: fully aware of how quickly computer technology has been evolving in the late twentieth century, the architects have designed flexible interior spaces to accommodate the ongoing revolution (on an almost monthly basis) in computer systems. For example, the cable shelves in the ceilings of the corridor and the hollow walls of the offices are designed to provide the easy access required by the constantly changing wiring requirements of the latest computer technology. No less practical than its neighbor on the other side of Olden Street, there is nevertheless a world of difference between the characterless E-Quad Cold Warrior to the east and the savvy information age Computer Science Building.

39. Engineering Quadrangle and Von Neuman Engineering Research Laboratory

Engineering Quadrangle *Voorhees, Walker, Smityh, and Haines, 1962*
Duffield Hall expansion *J. Robert Hillier, Hillier Group, 1993*
Von Neuman Engineering Research Laboratory *Sert, Jackson, and Associates, 1979*

Across Olden Street stands one of Princeton's least-loved building complexes, the Engineering Quadrangle, including Beggs, Maclean, Hayes, Bracket, and Duffield Halls. In 1979 the university expanded the quad to the east and south to include the Von Neuman Engineering Research Lab. Aesthetic judgments by the children of a previous generation are risky. The shifting fortunes of Princeton's Victorian architecture is a case in point. It was not that long ago that the prevailing wisdom dismissed Witherspoon dormitory and Alexander Hall as blots on the landscape. How much poorer the campus would be without them today.

That caveat notwithstanding, it is difficult to imagine that some future generation will embrace Princeton's E-Quad, or, as it formally known, the School of Engineering and Applied Science. Alien in concept and form to the rest of the campus, there is little about the original 1962 series of interconnected buildings (each named for distinguished faculty) wrapped around a central court that leads the eye forward or the spirit up. Like a mop and a bucket, the E-Quad with its 400 aluminum windows, 4,000 feet of corridors, 15,000 cinder blocks, and a half million bricks hung on the non-load-bearing curtain walls is resoundingly utilitarian. If Collegiate Gothic struggles to give the illusion of craftsmanship in a machine age, the architects of the Engineering Quad throw in the trowel. What results looks prefabricated. Nor did the architects seem concerned with relating the complex to the rest of the university.

Take the matter of how one approaches the E-Quad. If you draw a line that begins with Tiger Gate at the west, the complex sits at the eastern terminus of McCosh Walk. This is the last stop of *the* major east–west axis on campus. A Beaux Arts architect might have made a large gesture above the cornice—a gable or tower—something to catch the eye and pull the pedestrian forward. Instead, there is nothing to look at above the fascia of Beggs Hall, except a squat penthouse that hides mechanical equipment. Serviceable, yes, but dull and pedestrian. Or there might have been an arch that penetrated the building between Beggs and Maclean Halls, leading to a handsomely landscaped court.

There is in fact a surprise at the heart of the quad, a wonderfully landscaped garden with sculptures by Naum Gabo (*Spheric Theme*, stainless steel, 1973–74) and Masayuki Nagare (*Stone Riddle*, dark granite, 1967). But the way into the court summons no thanksgiving or praise. Instead, it is a secret garden entered almost surreptitiously, not from the west, which would have been a logical destination for McCosh Walk, but from the south by way of a parking lot. There is no ceremonial arch, merely a high-ceilinged passageway punched into the wall. Once inside the interior court, one is struck by a curious phenomenon: the rows of windows on all sides do not render the walls transparent as, say, the windows of the nineteenth-century East Pyne Hall on the main campus. For all the windows, the effect is dense and opaque. It is possible to enter the garden directly from the complex, but only from the second story and then down exterior stairs that are merely functional. Whether inside or out, the stairways of the E-Quad are treated as nothing more than prefabricated structural devices to take a person up or down. The garden, with its curved raised beds filled with a variety of deciduous and evergreen blooming shrubs and trees, is every-

Duffield Hall, Engineering Quadrangle

thing the surrounding architecture is not, right down to the different kinds
of gravel creatively used to define the ambling pathways. This improbable
patch of Eden is dedicated to the architect of the E-Quad, Stephen F.
Voorhees '00, a trustee and who, after Cram's resignation, was the university's Supervising Architect from 1930 to 1949.

A modest exception is the Engineering Library at the northwest cor-

Like the Pentagon, the E-Quad jealously guards its secrets. Inside
and out, the architecture provides few clues about how the 275,000 square
feet of classroom, laboratory, and office space are used. A visitor needs a
map to distinguish chemical engineering (Hayes Hall) from electrical engineering (Brackett Hall) from civil engineering (Maclean Hall). There are a
few saving graces: natural light is available to the offices on either side of
the double-loaded corridors thanks to the relative narrowness of the five
original halls, and the corridors are ample and well lit. But a walk through
the building still feels like a step back into a 1960s suburban high school.

A modest exception is the Engineering Library at the northwest corner facing out to Olden Street. The manufactured monochromatic brick of
the quad is abruptly punctuated by a blank limestone wall, which is itself
interrupted at the south end by a two-and-a-half-story expanse of plate
glass that signals the entrance. A flat metal canopy supported by four polished metal poles stretches over the entryway. Around the corner on the
north face, stone gives way to plate glass from the second story up, revealing students at work in a generously-sized reading room.

The west face of the library that one sees from the street sits at the
edge of that 1960s cliché—an elevated plaza. Perhaps responding to an
emptiness that even skillful plantings cannot hide, the plaza has acquired

Upstart II, a muscular piece of abstract art created by sculptor Clement Meadmore in 1970. In a setting of unyielding plain geometry, Meadmore's sculpture appears as frozen motion about to thaw: a giant black metal bar, which can be read as an abstract phallus, seems to be in the first split second of springing skyward away from an otherwise dispiriting space.

Robert Hillier's 1993 addition to Duffield Hall attempted to break out of the E-Quad's utilitarian mold. Although the street level of Hillier's addition is not much of an improvement on the blank torpor that afflicts the perimeter of the entire complex, above the first floor one discovers a stretching of the aesthetic palette as teal-colored window wedges jut out of an aubergine surface. Inside, Hillier called attention to a different design sensibility by literally pulling away the addition from the older structure. The resulting void creates a three-story atrium reaching to the clear glass tent of a skylight. Suddenly what had been a monotonous corridor in the older section of the complex now opens to diffused daylight, different textures and colors, and movement, as the paths of the connecting floors are revealed between the old structure and the new.

Two painted steel girders at cornice height span the north–south length of the atrium. Up to the first story of the base, the surface of Hillier's addition is glazed aubergine terra cotta block. These continue up and through the skylight on the north and south walls. Slate tiles are on the floor in two shades of gray and one of pink in a checkerboard pattern. The east wall of the atrium is punctuated by aubergine painted metal doors and window bays with teal-colored glass. The terra-cotta block along the east wall is capped by a wide limestone band, above which is apricot-colored brick. Overhead, two long white painted pipes that appear to carry the HVAC systems traverse the space from north to south. Just under the skylight, large cables are strung from girders to spread the weight load. The effect is both decorative and structural. Whereas the guts in that part of the complex designed by Voorhees are kept out of sight beneath drop ceilings and the like, the architect of the Duffield addition lets it all hang out. To be sure, exposed wires, ducts, cables, air returns, and exhausts as decorative elements were something of a contemporary cliché, yet appropriate in a building that celebrates the practical applied sciences.

40. Bowen Materials Institute *Alan Chimacoff, Hillier Group, 1993*

The new spirit that animates the Duffield addition fully resonates—and then some—in the Bowen Materials Institute, located south of the E-Quad on the other side of the parking lot. By contrast to E-Quad's secrecy, Bowen Hall is a bewilderingly exhibitionistic mix of colors, materials, and asymmetrical forms. The east facade is bracketed by two glass stairwells. On the opposite west side, the roof of the two-story bay functions as an outdoor terrace with tables and chairs for faculty and students. The south entrance opens into a foyer leading to a set of stairs immediately to the left, which turn back on themselves and out to an elevated atrium. The upper floors wrap around the atrium. The halls thus become in effect balconies. The entire space is lit by natural light that floods in through a skylight. You can see through to the north to a sculpture-like set of spiral stairs.

The exterior elevations are clad in blocks of burnt sienna terra cotta. Major variations on the primary rectilinear form, such as the expansive two-story semicircular bay on the west side, are faced with slabs of green granite. Stretched over the south and main entrance to the building is a simple steel canopy supported by a single polished steel girder, which when the sun strikes it looks electric. Acid-etched glazed tile interspersed with tiles of green granite are arranged in a grid above the entrance. The grid is tilted to form a mosaic of large diamond shapes that contrast with the prevailing horizontal bands of windows on this elevation. The operable windows appear like notes on a page of music, not repetitiously playing the same quarter time, but now half, now whole, now double rhythms. But this is not the music of a string quartet; rather, a brass band. The entrance is not square in the middle, but set off slightly to the left (a postmodern gesture a la Venturi), flanked by a pair of columns of contrasting shape, texture, and material. The undeniable busyness of the whole thing may be the architect's way of advertising that this is after all an academic facility dedicated to the study of materials.

Even though Chimacoff would appear to have gone off on a spending spree, what the architect is doing on both the interior and exterior of

Bowen Materials Institute

Bowen cannot be attributed solely to the generosity of the building's donor, Gordon Wu '58. Bowen Hall confirms the presence of a new sensibility reshaping this precinct of the Princeton campus, a sensibility that appears grounded in the theory of architect Robert Venturi, who applauds complexity and contradiction. However, as Chimacoff inadvertently makes clear, it is a sensibility that at times comes off more literary than architectural. Bowen, he writes, is an abstraction of materials science involving "purposeful ambiguity, where dissimilar or incompatible ideas and materials are brought together in ways that make them seem interchangeable: the inclusive or plausible oxymoron." Whether students and faculty are ready for oxymorons, plausible or otherwise, is another matter.

41. Ferris S. Thompson Gateway *McKim, Mead, and White, 1911*

Ferris S. Thompson Gateway

A brief detour immediately south of Bowen leads to a second example of McKim, Mead, and White's work on campus, the Ferris S. Thompson Gateway. Built when ceremonial gates seemed to be the rage on campuses all over America, this one seems somewhat marooned in its present location. Originally Thompson Gateway served as the entrance to the athletic fields, which were moved south in the 1950s to accommodate the construction of the Engineering Quad.

The existing wall in which this imposing ceremonial gate is set, begins to the west at the Third World Center (Thomas Oliphat Speir, 1890) on the northeast corner of Prospect Avenue and Olden Street and rises against the slope of Prospect, ultimately reaching a height of 20 feet when it arrives at the university's new parking garage. Of the two McKim, Mead, and White ceremonial gates on campus, this is arguably the more handsome, especially the floral elements that wriggle throughout the metal tracery, which is made to look delicate. If Vulcan had hammered out a bridal veil, this is what it might have looked like.

Thompson Gateway seems to want to be the south entrance to a quad that serves the applied sciences. But it stands too close to Bowen Hall. The tight siting preempts any future effort to use the gate to announce a major north–south axis from Prospect Avenue into the E-Quad. The gateway honors a track and field athlete from the class of 1888.

Parking Garage

Few demands are made of buildings that house a mundane service, such as a warehouse, a gas station, or a parking garage. The lie to this line of aesthetic reductionism is given resoundingly by Rodolfo Machado and Jorge Silvetti's inspired 410-car Parking Garage, which received an AIA Honor Award in 1993.

The first parking structure built on the university campus is part of a master plan for the Science and Engineering Quadrangle (also by the Boston firm of Machado and Silvetti, the university's current Consulting Architects). To design such a structure, the architects were challenged to define a building type destined to be more common on campus as academic buildings in this quadrant replace existing surface parking lots. Not only did they define but Machado and Silvetti elevated a utilitarian facility seldom associated with beauty or elegance into a delightful design.

Machado and Silvetti's parking structure adopts and extends the existing McKim, Mead, and White wall—which it relates to in height, texture, and materials. The building is constructed of a sand-polished, galvanized steel frame with poured-in-place concrete slabs. To complement and affirm the garden character of the surroundings, the three floors of the structure above the two-story brick wall are wrapped by a bronze lattice screen. Along the north side, the screen pulls free from the wall, creating a high arcade approximately ten feet wide that shelters an east–west path paved with the green slate common to Princeton's campus walks. The screen and the articulation of the design—the flared cornice, the flying buttress-like supports, the arcade and canopy along the north wall—impart an energy seldom associated with a parking garage. The shifting play of light and shadow alter the building's presence throughout the day.

Between the existing older wall and the parking structure, a new garden is created; here, on the southern side the architects clad the building in a green galvanized steel screen on which ivy climbs. Flanking the ivy wall, five-story copper panels identify the pedestrian entrances to the garage. In the middle of the south face, a two-story opening provides additional light and transparency to a building in which security and safety are essential. If the Engineering Quad drains all the artistry out of architecture and engineering, Machado and Silvetti pour the magic back in by an inspired use of common materials. What makes their accomplishment a *tour de force* is that they have discovered a certain poetry in the most pedestrian of modern building types—the urban parking garage.

Eating Clubs and Athletic Fields

East Campus

The story of the East Campus south of Prospect Avenue and the athletic fields is made up of three distinct narratives (or perhaps two plus a post-script): the Eating Clubs, the Athletic Facilities, and an academic beachhead between the two dedicated to mathematics and physics. Built at a furious pace within a relatively short period, the Prospect Avenue Eating Clubs are the oldest buildings on this Walk. The athletic facilities are among the most architecturally experimental facilities on campus. The math and physics quads come off as the most corporate.

Among the most outstanding groups of buildings at Princeton, the Eating Clubs do not have a formal relationship with the university. But no survey of the school's architecture would be complete without a brief look at the elite Prospect Avenue Eating Clubs. Ironically the splendid ensemble of buildings that makes this stretch of Prospect Avenue—otherwise known as *the Street*—may have had its origins in a food fight. If it was true that the sole purpose of a Princeton education was to prepare young men for the ministry, students might have tolerated with good grace the perennial scourge of campus life—poor food. But the student body in the last half of the nineteenth century was not exclusively (or even primarily) focused on spiritual nourishment. Growing in number, increasingly preoccupied with organized sports, and perpetually hungry, they were desperate for a dependable source of decent food. Further, the school's rural location meant fewer of the social diversions enjoyed by their peers at Columbia and Penn. Greek letter fraternities might have supplied both. However, they were formally banned in 1855.

Matters came to a head in 1877 when a group of Princeton's leading sophomores were denied access to their reserved table in the newly erected Commons. This suggests some sort of disturbance during one of the meals. Aggravating the problem was the fact that at this late point in the school term, there were few alternatives in this small town and they were booked up. If students were to eat, they had to rely on their own ingenuity. Thus the origins of the fateful decision to "buy a stove, hire a cook and set up a table in a room of Ivy Hall which was then vacant." Ivy Hall Eating Club was the first in what became a Princeton institution, unique in its power and prestige.

In the next four decades after Ivy Club purchased its first home on Prospect Avenue, the eating clubs developed into the remarkable collection of neo-Georgian, Gothic, and Colonial Revival buildings we see today. The architecture of the clubs suggests a privileged world of limited access, reinforced by the fact that the clubhouses could accommodate only between 20 and 40 upperclassmen. Students soon came to believe that an invitation to the right club was a passport to a golden future. In fact, membership did smooth the way for a seamless transition to the "Old Boy" network of prestigious metropolitan clubs in the downtowns of America's major cities. There was a time when the answer to the question, "And what Club did you belong to?" carried more weight than the simple fact of having a diploma. Sooner or later such a state of affairs was bound to concern those who considered the Clubs a challenge to the serious purpose of higher education. Woodrow Wilson, as the university president, was only the first who took on the powerful Eating Clubs—and only the first to lose.

This tension helps explain why over the course of the twentieth century the university has struggled to find a compelling alternative to the food and fellowship offered by the eating clubs. It is perhaps no accident that Princeton's new multi-million dollar Frist Student Center, under construction as this book is being written, will be located within sight of Prospect Avenue. As of last count, there are eleven private clubs in operation.

43. Ivy Club *Cope and Stewardson, 1896*

Ivy Club

The obvious place to begin is with Ivy, reputedly modeled on Peacock Inn, a seventeenth-century Gothic building in Derbyshire (a picture of which hangs inside the Club). If proof is needed to show that the Eating Clubs are an integral thread in the university's architectural warp and woof, Ivy provides the compelling evidence. In the very year Ivy retained Cope and Stewardson (1896), the firm was at work on Blair Hall, the first and arguably the signature Collegiate Gothic structure on campus. As William K. Selden notes in his excellent history of club life, the completion of the new clubhouse for Ivy "added immeasurably to the growing reputation of Princeton as an institution of exceptional privilege." From the standpoint of the university's trustees and many influential donors, the clubs were a splendid advertisement for the school.

Cope and Stewardson's work for what F. Scott Fitzgerald called a "detached and breathlessly aristocratic" club was not the firm's sole venture into domestic architecture in the Princeton area, but Ivy was their only club. No doubt the students and their well-heeled alumni members were able to land this prize catch because the firm was working on Constitution Hill, the Princeton mansion of clubman Junius S. Morgan (class of 1888), a nephew of J. Pierpont Morgan. The Constitution Hill connection is important because both buildings are skillful exercises in domestic Tudor Gothic architecture. Indeed, the same wine dark rough red brick, interspersed with black and forest green, is used in both. The divisions between the floors is articulated on the exterior by stone string courses. The grouped perpendicular-style brick chimneys rising above the third floor of the gabled green slate roof, the dark green trim of the recessed leaded windows framed in red sandstone, the three finials that crown the entry doorway, and the irregular massing suggesting growth over time—each element contributes to the overall comfortable clubbiness.

A walk around to the back reveals a more informal elevation. The most notable element is a large gambrel-roofed wing that houses the dining room and kitchen. Whether front or back, the choice of style and the deft execution of its construction instantly convey a sense of permanence and long-standing tradition, remarkable when one considers that the club itself was barely twenty years old.

44. Cottage Club *McKim, Mead, and White, 1906*

Cottage Club

Cope and Stewardson's architectural *coup de force* was bound to provoke the particular envy of the neighbors who were housed in a shingled frame building immediately to the east, Cottage Club. Organized in 1886 as "The Seven Wise Men of Grease," the second oldest eating club had its origins in a saloon on Nassau Street across from the campus. When in 1892, Club members followed the example of Ivy and built their own house on Prospect Avenue, the pattern for the future development of the street had been set. It took club members and their wealthy alumni (most notably the Palmer family) another ten years after Ivy had raised the bar before Cottage was prepared to trump their rivals. And so they did with a stunning Georgian Revival house designed by no lesser a talent than Charles McKim (1847–1909), a partner of America's premiere architectural firm, McKim, Mead, and White, the very firm that had just remodeled the White House (1903) and had designed the impressive new gateway in front of Nassau Hall.

Frank Lloyd Wright once said that buildings either sit or stand on the land. Whereas the architecture of Ivy might be described as sitting (and deliberately so), McKim, Mead, and White's brick clubhouse clearly stands. Derisively called "The White Elephant of Prospect Street" (by its neighbors no doubt), this most expensive of the upper-class eating clubs was immediately perceived as the most luxurious and hence privileged right down to the private tennis court at the back. It certainly appealed to F. Scott Fitzgerald whose years as a member of Cottage contributed to the authenticity of his literary renderings of America's golden lads and lasses.

The footprint of Cottage traces a U-shape plan, with the arms of the U extending south. It is worth the walk down Roper Lane past a great lush hedge of holly to fully appreciate the sense of privilege the architecture con-veyed to Cottage Club members and their guests. At the rear, pairs of french doors open out to a court at the front of which extends a Doric columned loggia that connects both arms of the U. Steps lead down to what had been the tennis court, but which is now a pleasant formal boxwood garden whose flanking gravel paths terminate at a pair of pavilions that face one another.

At the front, the formal or more public face of the building is an essay in self-confident balance and symmetry, which stands in deliberate contrast to the sharp angles and shadowy irregularity of Ivy next door. On either end of the facade, a broad bay projects ever so slightly to the east and west, relaxing somewhat the Club's formal public face. The entrance is a wide pavilion that makes a modest step forward from the facade. The rounded transom of the entry door is echoed by the expansive elliptical pedi-ment that caps the pavilion on either side of which are a pair of dormers that follow the curve of the roof. The diamond-patterned brick of the elliptical space between the second story and the roof line is pierced at the center by an elliptical oculus whose glass is in turn divided by elliptical mullions. The primary architectural elements of the entry pavilion and rectangular corner bays are edged in white quoins and the division between the first and second floor is outlined by a string course. Above each of the windows of the first two stories, white keystones anchor the brick arches. The slate of the roof is a handsome pattern of gray and red, crowned by an elegant widow's walk.

Inside, the elegance continues. The hall floors are laid with stone and the walls lined with wood paneling, both imported from England. The library is a copy taken from Oxford's Merton College. The U-shaped plan and the abundance of large windows on all sides ensure that the spacious, well-proportioned rooms are flooded by an abundance of natural light. Perhaps the most telling detail is the Latin proverb inscribed over the fire-place in the Club's dining room: "*Ubi Amici Ibindem Sunt Opes*" ["Where there are friends, there are also riches"].

The year after Cottage opened, President Wilson, who had himself approved the plans for the new clubhouse, announced his intention to shut down the eating clubs. In his eyes they were anti-democratic and anti-intel-lectual. What had begun a few decades earlier as an innocent solution in the pursuit of a nourishing dinner had, to Wilson and other critics of the clubs, become a distraction at odds with an ideal community of scholars. Ironically, the visible splendor of clubs like Cottage and Ivy, with all the riches and privilege the architecture seemed to imply, became a rallying point for those opposed then and in later years to the very idea of the exclu-sivity and privilege they seemed to imply.

If Ivy and Cottage represent to high water mark, they by no means exhaust the architectural delight in store for the visitor to Prospect Avenue. At the risk of over-simplification, the architecture communicates three dis-tinct messages about power, each one embodied by a particular style: Gothic

(Anglo-Saxon, Protestant, aristocratic), Georgian (urbane, moneyed), and Colonial (suburban, country club). Common to all three styles is the message that these are the nurseries of and the thresholds into the *Establishment*.

45. Dial Lodge and Colonial Club

Dial Lodge   *Henry Milliken, 1917*
Colonial Club   *Robert Gibson and Francis G. Stewart '86, 1907*

Colonial Club

Before walking south from Prospect toward the athletic facilities, the remaining fourteen clubhouses on or near The Street merit a passing glance. At the northeast corner of Prospect Avenue and Washington Road is Dial Lodge designed by Henry Milliken. The architect's use of Princeton's official Collegiate Gothic style and the choice of the descriptive noun "lodge" over the word "club" were conscious efforts to deflect the charges of elitism Wilson and others had leveled at the Clubs. No longer a private club, Dial will be the future home of the new Bendheim Center for Finance. One hopes that the signature sundial will remain above the front door. Next door, Colonial Club's bold, overscaled entry portico supported by four massive Ionic columns anchors a raised porch from which the social functions of Club members can be observed by passersby on the street who are not members. The porch is thus the stage on which privilege is played, and passerby on the sidewalk are the audience.

46. Tiger Inn and Elm Club

Tiger Inn   *G. Howard Chamberlin, 1895*
Elm Club   *Raleigh C. Gildersleeve, 1901; major alterations, 1930–1931*

Reflecting the epidemic Anglophilia of the day, the architect of Tiger Inn is said to have been inspired by a half-timbered old English tavern from the Chelsea section of London. Tiger might well be called the house of many gables. This, and the distinctive overhanging second-story, convey domesticity . The last club on this side of the street is Elm, a Tuscan revival structure. As originally designed, Elm was the sole exercise in the Italianate style among the Prospect Eating Clubs. But the redesign undertaken in 1930–31 stripped away most of the characteristic Florentine features, such as Gildersleeve's hipped roof with its projecting eaves. A wing added on the east side absorbs most of what had been a covered porch that ran around the base. The impulse behind the 1930s redesign seems to have been an attempt to give the club a modern, streamlined face. True, the result does look like an exercise in the vocabulary of early art moderne, but the effect suggests a facelift that has gone bad. Never the most architecturally distinguished building on the block, Elm has lost much of the character it once had. And the macadam parking lot that fills up the backyard does not help.

47. Court Club and Key and Seal

Court Club *1927; 1955–1957*
Key and Seal *Walter H. Jackson, 1924*

Crossing Prospect to the south side, the Walk continues from the east back toward Washington Road, beginning with Court, a brick Collegiate Gothic building with two asymmetrical flanking wings (one hipped, the other gabled), and Key and Seal, also a Collegiate Gothic design executed in brick and limestone. Among the last clubs to be built on Prospect, the understated entrances of both strike a common, more modest note than the braggadocio of earlier clubs, such as Colonial and Cottage. Of the two, Key and Seal makes the more lasting impression. It is a seemingly effortless exercise in breaking down a large volume into agreeable parts. The three-story off-center gabled wing, for example, the varied roof heights, the stepped-out eave over the porch, and the rounded bay at the northwest corner add dimension and contribute to the domestic scale. Either building would fit in comfortably with the undergraduate dormitories the university was building around the same time. No longer private operations, both clubs have been run by the university since 1972 as the Adlai E. Stevenson Hall for upper-class dining.

48. Charter Club *Arthur Meigs '03, 1914*

There is no such reticence about the elegant Georgian Revival silhouette cut by Charter Club. Architectural historians Constance Greif and William Short describe the club of literary critic Edmund Wilson ('16) and actor James Stewart ('32) as "a prime example of the Colonial Revival movement in the style of a stone eighteenth-century Philadelphia Georgian mansion such as those in Fairmont Park." The limestone cartouche that rises above and breaks the entry pediment, the curve of which is echoed in the Palladian window above, forecasts the future rewards that await the suburban banker and his family. Charter is precisely the to-the-manor-born estate that a moneyed Main Line clientele would buy from their Philadelphia architect. Among the many graceful elements that distinguish this structure is the granite stone facing, rich in sparkling mica, and the gently flared pitch of the red and green slate roof.

49. Cloister Inn and Cap and Gown

Cloister Inn *R. H. Scannell, 1924*
Cap and Gown *Raleigh C. Gildersleeve, 1907*

A building that appears to belong on a university campus is the aptly named Cloister Inn, executed in Collegiate Gothic. The geometry of the triangle prevails in this design. Only the necklace of hipped dormers and the absence of overt Christian imagery signal that this long, low stone structure with its pointed-arched windows (continuing around the building to frame a covered patio on the west side) is not in fact a rural Anglican church. The single bold gesture would have to be the powerful vertical thrust of the enormous grouped chimneys with their plump caps. The energy of the north and west sides seems to give out at the rear, which is plain and stuccoed. The architectural stakes are raised much higher by the Gothic-styled Cap and Gown. The dark three-story brick facade, with its distinctive ogee-arched entry, sports some of the most elaborate exterior detailing on the street, in particular the window arrangement of the eastern ell that projects out toward Prospect. A feature unique to Cap and Gown is the double diamond stringcourse that indicates the interior division between the first and second floors. The double diamond pattern is repeated in the chimney.

50. Quadrangle Club and Cannon Club

Quadrangle Club *Henry O. Milliken '05, 1916*
Cannon Club *Edgar V. Seeler, 1910*

Skipping Cottage and Ivy, the next stop is Quadrangle Club. Quadrangle illustrates the risk inherent in calling on a trustee to design your Club: what one may save in architectural fees may diminish a client's right to be appropriately critical. Milliken attempted the self-assured elegance of the Georgian revival manner, right down to a noble portico with its broken pediment (a deliberate echo of Westover, a well-known Tidewater Virginia plantation). But the over-scaled portico does not quite fit with the facade, which appears more relentless than symmetrical. The string of small second-story windows and the lack of dormers facing the street call too much attention to the horizontal emphasis, creating the impression of a flat stageset rather than a three-dimensional building.

If the architect of Quadrangle reaches beyond his grasp, Cannon attempts far less, but accomplishes a bit more. Of all the clubs, its facade is the most understated. In fact, apart from the obviously Gothic entrance, it is hard to discern just what stylistic manner that architect intended for the front elevation. What many passersby remember is not the building, but the artillery piece in the front lawn. Cannon can be best appreciated by walking around back or stepping inside. Seen from the rear, the main body of

Cannon is an asymmetrical, three-story elevation with a single-story kitchen wing on the east side. Whereas the slate roof at the front is penetrated by three modest shed dormers, the rear reveals large, ecclesiastical windows framed by two clipped gable roofs of different heights. Inside, a massive medieval fireplace provides a dramatic focus to the two-story living room. Along with its signature field piece and its justly acclaimed hearth, Cannon has an additional claim in the history books: it was the first club faced in native stone. Sold to the university in 1974, Cannon has been extensively remodeled inside—rechristened Notestein Hall—and currently houses the Office of Population Research.

51. Tower Club, Campus Club, and Terrace Club

Tower Club   *Roderic Barnes, 1917*
Campus Club   *Raleigh C. Gildersleeve, 1909*
Terrace Club   *Frederick Stone, remodeling, 1920s*

The steeply pitched roofs, irregular massing, and crenellated towers of Tower and Campus invite the observer to regard both clubs as an extension of the university, since both are constructed of the same dark brick and limestone trim as Princeton's Palmer and 1879 Halls just across Washington Road. Down the street to the south stands the half-timbered Terrace, which occupies the residence of John Grier Hibben, who had lived there in the years before he succeeded Wilson as president (1912–1932). Rather than razing the house for a new structure, the members moved into the building right after the club was founded. Over time they reconfigured the Hibben residence beyond all recognition. Thus Terrace can make the claim that it is singular among the eating clubs in that still occupies the first clubhouse it purchased, albeit through an act of assimilation that rendered the original structure invisible.

52. Center for Jewish Life   *Robert A. M. Stern, 1993*

A postscript to The Street stands south of Terrace on Washington Road, the ochre and brown Center for Jewish Life. In recent years, past anti-Semitic practices have been challenged and largely routed by students, faculty, and the Princeton administration. A measure of this change is the Center for Jewish Life, which operates under the Office of the Dean of Religious Life, and is staffed by a university administrator and B'nai B'rith Hillel foundation.

Robert Stern (1939–), the Dean of Yale's Architecture School, was an excellent choice for a project conceived to relate architecturally and culturally to the tradition-bound eating clubs. No living American architect has a greater understanding of domestic design in this country during the late-nineteenth and early-twentieth centuries than Stern. It is a talent that has been known to drive contemporary modernists up the wall. And no architect is more capable of pouring the old wine into new bottles in ways that do not come off as skilled forgeries or mere pastiche. Whether Stern is totally successful at Princeton may be another question.

Built to accommodate the social, educational, religious, and dietary needs of Princeton's Jewish community, the Center conveys the air of being a long-time neighbor, rather than an interloper, right down to the copper standing-seam roof, the look of which recalls traditional slate of neighboring clubs. Other familiar elements from the Prospect Avenue streetscape include asymmetrical massing, mullioned windows, hipped dormers, a classical arrangement of windows (larger at the base to smaller in the upper stories), and massive chimneys that render functional elements ornamental. Like McKim's Cottage Club, the formal entry off Washington Road stands in sharp contrast to a more relaxed, heavily fenestrated and terraced space that opens not at the back, which is a service area, but to the south and ample sun. An additional advantage of the southern exposure is a long view down the slope of the land of the athletic fields and new stadium. Again, like McKim, Stern uses the site's gentle, downward slope to enhance the privileged texture of this space, adding a great eyebrow dormer that gazes out toward Lake Carnegie.

This dormer, along with other visual clues, gives away Stern's sources: whereas the gentile clients of Prospect relentlessly pursued English models around the turn of the twentieth century, the architect of the Center for Jewish Life reaches back to roughly the same period and grounds his building in indigenous "American" period styles, from shingle style to prairie, with arts-and-crafts doors and Viennese secession lamp fixtures. But the eclectic melange seems a bit too self-conscious for its own good.

Center for Jewish Life

In developing a design vocabulary for residential, academic, and religious buildings, Princeton's architects had a rich tradition to draw on. Designing athletic facilities was a different matter. There was little contemporary precedent in Europe or America for buildings whose primary function was to accommodate athletics and physical fitness. Indeed, until about the mid-nineteenth century, organized sports were actively discouraged by Princeton's faculty and trustees. Most educators dismissed sports as mere games; certainly not the business of serious young men.

Here as elsewhere it was the transformational force of James McCosh that set Princeton on a different course and in 1869 resulted in the construction of Bonner Gymnasium on the western edge of campus. However, what was deservedly hailed as the first large gymnasium built by any American college became in less than three decades hopelessly inadequate. Not only was the student body larger, most undergraduates participated in one sport or another, a tradition that continues today with a level of student involvement greater than any other Ivy League school.

With few examples of what a gymnasium should look like, architects focused on the utilitarian need for durability, flexibility, and space. They then wrapped the whole package in one of the popular revivalist modes. The architect of Bonner set the precedent by designing essentially a large masonry shed decked out in Romanesque clothes, dressed up with a pair of flanking polygonal stair towers on the south side. In 1903 the school opened a new Gymnasium (at that time the largest in the country) below Blair and Stafford Little Halls. Although finely crafted (the handsome Trophy Room at the front was paneled in English Oak), the building not surprisingly was really little more than a spacious warehouse, this time a la Collegiate Gothic.

Indeed, if there was any new precedent being created, it was the American rage for organized collegiate athletics and the increasing need to build ever bigger and ever more flexible facilities to accommodate the increasing number of sports and the players, as well as the growing number of fans. Initially, architects did not reach for new forms, but occupied themselves with facilities that blended in with the surrounding campus as if to say physical fitness is now a healthy part of the college experience. Imitation was not simply flattery, but a necessary defensive strategy, like a guest at a fancy dress dinner who, not sure which piece of flatware to reach for, keeps his eye on the host. Sooner or later, however, it was bound to occur to architects that a building type without a history was a blank slate inviting innovation. Also, college athletics had come out of the closet in a big way. Like it or not, admissions officers discovered that a winning basketball team put a school on the map. Their colleagues in the development office simultaneously discovered a rich source of revenue.

53. Jadwin Gymnasium *Steinmann, Cain, and White, 1969*

Jadwin Gymnasium

Jadwin Gymnasium marks a definite stage in the evolutionary process that had its origins more than a century earlier on the grass of Cannon Green. Two things strike one about Jadwin on a first encounter: it is like nothing else on campus and it is BIG—so big that it is only from the air that one can appreciate its unique, three-part cantilevered roof and geodesic construction on which is stretched a rubberized fabric. A product of modern engineering and construction techniques, Jadwin looks as if it could be telescoped into a larger or smaller shape, depending on the need. But "smaller" in this context is a relative word. Jadwin is a product of an era in which communities and campuses across the country were constructing mega, multi-purpose facilities that could quickly and inexpensively squeeze in a wide range of spectator sports from badminton to baseball, from basketball to hockey. Such multi-purpose facilities tend to be engineering marvels rather than aesthetic delights. For one thing, the Brobdinagian scale is off-putting.

However, the point of Jadwin is to accommodate practice, performance, and participation. It does all three quite well, providing state-of-the-art facilities for basketball, fencing, squash, tennis, wrestling, track, and many other field sports on its two main levels. Seating 7,500, the main auditorium on the first level can easily provide the critical mass for rock and pop concerts. Permanent seats are limited to one side, which permits the open space to be configured either as a theater with seats in one direction or a court. Jadwin was also among the first campus buildings whose design was shaped by the university's decision to go coed. Locker rooms for women's teams were an integral part of the original plan.

There is a bronze statue against the west wall of the lobby that commemorates an earlier chapter in Princeton's history. Variously called the *Christian Student* or the *Christian Athlete*, the statue is the work of the sculptor, Daniel Chester French (1850–1931), best known for the seated Abraham Lincoln in Washington, D.C.'s Lincoln Memorial. It memorializes W. Earl Dodge Jr., a founding leader of the Intercollegiate Young Men's Christian Association. Initially located (appropriately) near Dodge Hall on the main campus, the *Christian Student* was not surprisingly the target of student pranks, until the university removed this source of aggravation by lending it to the Daniel Chester French Museum in Stockbridge, Massachusetts. The good offices of a Princeton alumnus secured its return and installation in Jadwin, where it presumably has come to permanent rest.

54. DeNunzio Pool and Caldwell Field House

DeNunzio Pool   *Craig Mullins and Cesar Pelli, 1990*
Caldwell Field House   *Steinmann, Cain, and White, 1963*

The apparent straightforward design of DeNunzio deserves a second glance. It shows how a creative architect can use the simplest gestures to break up what is finally a box that contains a 50-meter Olympic size pool and bleachers to accommodate 1,300 spectators. Consider the shape of the copper downspouts and how they are arranged across the three planes of the front elevation. They suggest ascending rows of colonnades. Consider the three planes, which break up the basic rectangle and give the structure a vertical thrust. Consider how color, both as a field or background (red brick at the lower stories, teal at the top) and as visual punctuation (the groupings of dark red tile by the downspouts and the rich copper of the downspouts themselves) imparts a pleasing texture to what is functionally a glorified shed. Like a few dabs of makeup, these are simple but deft applications that make all the difference.

55. Palmer Stadium   *Rafael Vinoly, 1998–1999*

Without question the crown jewel of the East Campus athletic precinct is the university's new Palmer Stadium. As the campus' first building of the twenty-first century, it marks an auspicious beginning. Princeton's twentieth-century athletic facilities were in essence decorated sheds; their architects had few contemporary models to steer their course. Yet there was one older tradition, the Roman amphitheater, which offered a functional and monumental reference and exerted an increasingly powerful influence with the rise of university-sanctioned field sports, football most especially. The blatant classical overtones served to add the sanction of a noble tradition to what a few generations earlier would have been dismissed as the idle play of boys. The distance covered by what had been "idle play" can be measured by the fact that Princeton chose Henry Hardenbergh (1847–1918), the architect of Manhattan's luxurious Plaza hotel, to design its first stadium, a 46,000-seat facility. Hardenbergh pulled off the feat in seven months, in time for the Princeton–Dartmouth game. Dartmouth (thankfully) lost.

Not a true amphitheater, Palmer Stadium (named after its principal benefactor) was shaped like a horseshoe, open at the south. A hybrid of modern construction technology (reinforced concrete), classical in spirit, and Gothic in detail with buttresses, turrets, and a pointed arch facing the main approach from Roper Lane, Palmer rapidly acquired the aura of sacred ground. It also had a very un-sacred need for constant repair, a legacy no doubt of the rush to completion. Ultimately the unthinkable prevailed:

Palmer Stadium had to be replaced. It is a testament to Rafael Vinoly's achievement that the replacement he designed was immediately embraced by students, athletes, and alumni alike as if Palmer Stadium had died and rose transfigured from the mud of the construction site.

In an era when "big" is inevitably succeeded by "jumbo," as if size alone were a measure of progress, Vinoly did the unexpected: he shrunk the new $45-million facility from Palmer's 46,000 seats to 30,000 seats. This is in part achieved by locating the track, which had been inside Palmer Stadium, immediately to the south where it is joined to the stadium by back-to-back stands. The result is greater intimacy, enhanced by the fact that the field itself is sunken, which has the effect of placing the spectator closer to the action. Vinoly follows Palmer's horseshoe footprint, but closes the south end with movable grandstands.

The outer wall of the new stadium is a load-bearing structural concrete block with a brushed gravel aggregate surface. The aggregate itself is made up of bits of stone whose palette runs from amber to green and small flecks of black, which serve to soften the reflected light. A press box, offices, rest rooms, concessions, and conference rooms are located within the wall, which is pierced by a regular rhythm of large, razor-edged openings. The alternating pattern of masonry and sharply-incised voids allows Vinoly to call the structure a *colonnade*. Because the grandstands hang from the so-called colonnade, supported by a system of trusses, these penetrations are not visible from the inside of the stadium, with the notable exceptions at the northeast and northwest corners of the U. Here there is no upper seating. Instead, at either side there is a great portal made up of a central monumental square flanked by two equally monumental rectangles. The effect is a wonderful exercise in playing off mass against void.

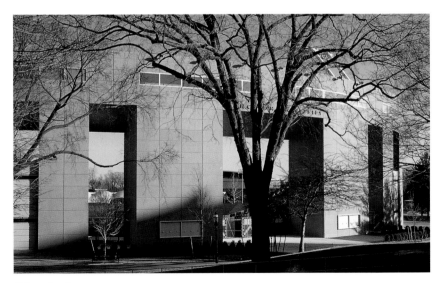

Palmer Stadium

Bleachers' structure, Palmer Stadium

The lesson is further enriched by the way the structure absorbs sunlight, particularly in the early morning and the late afternoon, when rays of light rake across the surface and passages of the colonnade.

Crowds enter these great portals onto Caldwell or Colman Plazas and then proceed into Palmer Pavilion, a ground-level concourse. The gates are decorated by slightly abstracted square interpretation of the university's shield, which carries the familiar motto, "*Vet Nov Testamentum*," the "Old and New Testaments." From here you can continue along the concourse to a seat in the lower grand stands or climb (there are elevators) to a mezzanine that runs along the inside of Vinoly's colonnade for access to a higher seat. To get from the mezzanine to the various sections of upper seating, you walk across one of the skywalks that are suspended from pairs of cables attached to the trusses. Hung rather than supported, the grandstands seem to float. In the campus precinct that houses the Engineering School, the inherent art of engineering is realized not in the architecture of the E-Quad, but here, on Princeton's playing fields.

56. Jadwin Hall, Fine Hall, and McDonnell Hall

Jadwin Hall   *Hugh Stubbins Associates, 1968*
Fine Hall   *Warner, Burns, Toan, and Lunde, 1968*
McDonnell Hall   *Gwathmey and Siegel, 1998*

Continuing west toward Washington Road, one comes to a complex of three academic halls: Jadwin, Fine, and McDonnell. The trio of facilities and the two quadrangles they define seem less a part of the East Campus than an extension or spilling over of the academic precinct on the other side of Washington Road. But Jadwin along with Fine can be considered the definitive close of an aesthetically dithering chapter on the East Campus, opened nearly two decades earlier by the architects of Corwin Hall. True, some of the sterile ambiance of a mid-twentieth-century corporate office park infuses the area, right down to the commissioned Alexander Calder stabile, *Five Disks: One Empty* (1969), on the plaza between Fine and Jadwin. But corporate or no, the architects can be credited for a certain boldness as well as their use of precedents that worked well in Princeton's pre-Cold War architecture.

Take the high-rise that anchors the western corner of Fine Hall. It is a building students love to hate. Thirteen stories in all (a ten-story tower standing atop a horizontal three-story base), Fine is a classic collection of 1960s clichés—tower on columns (*piloti*) perched on a low slab that abuts a plaza. Clichés notwithstanding, the design has a logical relationship to the rest of the campus. Like Holder Tower at the northwest corner of the university or Cram's great Cleveland Tower at the Graduate College, Fine Hall is a point of reference, announcing the campus to anyone approaching from the south along Washington Road. Also, unlike the relentless ground-hugging Engineering Quad, the vertical organization of activity in Fine minimizes the footprint of the structure on the land.

Clad in dark honey-brown granite, both the tower and base of Fine Hall are free of any ornament. This, however, does not mean a lack of surface interest. The architects break up the exterior planes of the curtain walls to good effect (in particular the chamfered corners and the bands of recessed windows), imparting a texture that shifts as the light changes. Yes, the tower is too short for its width. It comes off heavy despite the various attempts to break up the surface geometry. Yet this is a modern building. The top has to look as if a sharp knife had lopped it off. And, even those who have little affection for the exterior of the tower admit that the people inside like the views. Work spaces have a certain intimacy because the building is arranged vertically instead of strung out.

An historic footnote: the complex is named in honor of Henry Burchard Fine (1858–1928), first dean of the Department of Science. Fine became Dean of the Faculty under Woodrow Wilson in 1903. Together the two worked to raise the university's academic standards. It was on Fine's watch that Princeton became a leading center for the study of mathematics, attracting such international luminaries as Albert Einstein, who had an office in what is today Jones Hall. Carved in German over the fireplace in the common room are his words: "Cunning is the Lord God, but malicious

Jadwin Hall

Jadwin Hall, left; *Fine Hall's tower,* right

He is not." Sir Jacob Epstein's bronze of Einstein (1933) is located in the Fine Hall Library.

South of Fine, and defining the opposing edge of an open quad-rangle or plaza, is the six-level granite and brown brick Jadwin Hall. Within Jadwin is a second, closed quadrangle or courtyard, in which stands Antoine Pevsner's bronze, *Construction in the Third and Fourth Dimension* (1962).

Although the architect does not employ a ceremonial arch or gateway to guide pedestrian traffic in and out of the courtyard, the spaces are visually connected, if somewhat hard-edged and austere. There is also a spacious underground connection between Jadwin and Fine, which serves as the library for both the math and physics departments. In fact, it turns out the plaza is really the roof of the library, which explains why the landscaping is not grass and flowers, but crushed red stone. The single tree—a large pine at the northern edge—rises from a spacious light well. Looking down into the well or through the glass of Fine Hall, which defines the north edge of the well, you can see into the library. Outside the library is Arnaldo Pomodoro's polished bronze, *Sphere VI* (1966).

The most recent building in the math/physics complex is McDonnell Hall. Functionally an addition to Jadwin, McDonnell is used as a teaching facility, providing classrooms and laboratories for undergraduate physics and math classes. The building strikes a much different note from the rigid geometry of this gold-red-brown precinct. If a buttoned-down building like Jadwin Hall could take an acid trip, McDonnell would be the fractured result. From the bold blue square column that holds up the entry canopy to the collision of the different geometries that intersect at various points in the structure, McDonnell is an act of deconstruction. The contrast is a shorthand lesson in how a building of the 1990s is different from one designed thirty years earlier. For all their creativity, architects are no more likely to escape their era than anyone else.

For instance, in common with many buildings designed from roughly 1950 into the 1970s, Jadwin and Fine Halls are infatuated with one particular geometric shape—the rectangle, whether it is put flat on the ground or stood up on its narrow edge or run in strip windows around the perimeter. God may be in the details, but the details always seem to be right angles. Also, once a particular material is chosen, architects of this period tend to use the same material throughout—front, back, sides, and even inside. By contrast, like their Victorian predecessors, architects of the 1990s favor variety in color, materials, and shapes. No two sides of McDonnell are the same. In part, that is dictated by how the space is used inside. For example, the laboratory classrooms are located on the west side of the building and it is this elevation that features the most windows set in broad bands in a series of three slanting silver-gray metallic ribbed bays or wedges that angle out from the plane of the west facade like the half-open drawers of a bedroom dresser. If metal cladding is one sure sign of the 1990s, so is the use of glass block and blonde wood along with a tendency to expose the heating, ventilation, and cooling systems as part of the decor.

The east elevation of McDonnell, the side that faces and encloses the quad formed by Jadwin and Fine, is a beige-colored rusticated cast-stone wall. If the side facing Washington Road is restless, this interior elevation has the perverse effect of intensifying the feeling of the plaza as a cold, hard-edged space. Walking up the stairs that lead onto the plaza from the east, one sees little more than that wall, with the exception of the curious metal pyramid on the roof that appears to be part of the ventilation system. It is a delightful touch, but neither the wall nor the blue column is able to overcome the pedestrian's experience of coming to a dead end.

57. Palmer Hall/Frist Campus Center

Henry Janeway Hardenbergh, 1908; Venturi Scott Brown, 1999

At this writing, Palmer and the area around it are a construction site. In the process of a major redesign by Venturi Scott Brown, Palmer and the surrounding open space are undergoing a metamorphosis from the former home of the physics department to what will be called the Frist Campus Center. For most of its history, Princeton has been a step behind the expanding living and social needs of its students. In the early days of the College of New Jersey, Whig and Clio Halls were founded by students to meet pressing needs that were not being addressed by college administrators, including access to an adequate library. Later, toward the end of the nineteenth century, the Prospect Avenue eating clubs arose in response to the lack of dependably good food. That and opportunities to socialize.

When Frist Campus Center opens in fall of 2000, it will be the first time that Princeton will have a state-of-the-art social facility for all students. Whether Frist will complement or subvert the nearby eating clubs will turn as much on the university's intent as it will the amenities of the Campus Center. At its most benign, the siting of Frist simply acknowledges that the center of the campus is no longer Cannon Green. In fact, Cram's 1925 Master Plan anticipated this growth of the campus to the east and south and proposed a "University Club" for upperclassmen on the northeast corner of Prospect Avenue and Washington Road, where the Woodrow Wilson School of Public and International Affairs stands today. If the university does intend to co-opt the Clubs, this is precisely the site to throw down the gauntlet.

The Venturi Scott Brown redesign calls for the present oblong 1879 Green to be the new tree-shaded heart of the campus, with Frist Center anchoring the south end. The 1879 Green will follow the slope of the land and step down on the north side to the main entrance of the Frist Center. The architects' affection for well-defined front doors—oblique ones in this case—will be realized here through the creation of a freestanding limestone and brick arcade, approximately 17 feet tall, designed to frame and focus the entrance. The arcade does not run the full length of the front, but begins on the east side of the west pavilion and runs past the eastern edge of the building. What may seem arbitrarily off-center in plan will likely make sense when one approaches the entrance from the north across the Green. On the other hand, the design might well turn out to be more of Venturi exhibiting his knowledge of architectural history. As seen in Wu Hall, Venturi is a master at applying traditional forms unconventionally.

With the exception of that arcade and major exterior work on the south side facing Guyot Hall, the design strategies are primarily a matter of interior architecture to accommodate the building's totally new program. The upper levels will include a lecture hall, classrooms, a theater, and the renowned Gest Oriental Library, already located in Palmer. Offices for student organizations will be here as well. Below the building's original ground floor, down an expansive open central staircase, will be the Center's Commons area, which will function as a sort of enclosed village with three "streets"—home to a convenience store, copy center, a video-rental outlet, ATM machines, a pub, cafe, mailboxes, and a lounge. Because the land slopes steeply, the next floor down will be dining space that will open out to the south lawn that stretches toward Guyot Hall.

The three-story Tudor Gothic building Hardenburgh designed has until now been more distinguished for the Nobel Prize winners who have worked inside its efficient and practical spaces—with two important exceptions: the pair of larger-than-life size statues that flank the main north entrance. Sculpted by Daniel Chester French, they depict two outstanding American scientists, Benjamin Franklin (1706–1790) and Princeton's own Joseph Henry (1797–1878). In their role as sentries to Princeton's new Campus Center, they will usher in an era that is bound to have a major impact on Prospect Avenue and the entire Princeton University campus.

South Campus

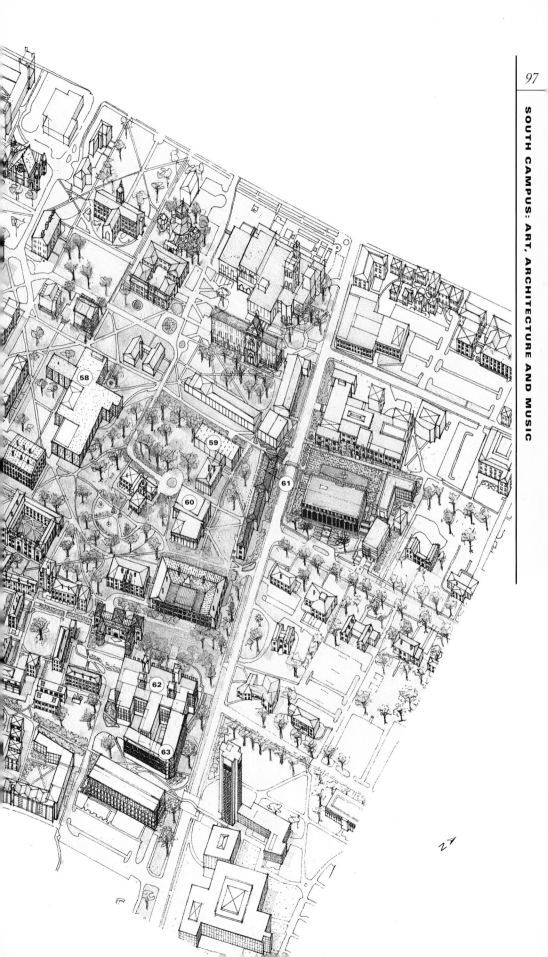

The story of the campus south of McCosh Walk and west of Washington Road is bracketed by a railroad and a lake. The railroad is the spur of the main line that runs between Philadelphia and New York, otherwise known as the "Dinky" or the PJ&B—Princeton Junction and Back. The lake is Andrew Carnegie's monumental watery offering to Princeton, a gift that came about after a ride on the Dinky.

It is hard to overstate the impact of the railroad on Princeton's south campus. After the Civil War, the primary approach to the college was by rail. The siting of Witherspoon dormitory on a rise looking over the train station, as well as its prominence, was meant to impress parents, students, and potential donors as they drew within sight of the campus. Later, the crenellated towers of Blair Hall served the same purpose. Blair Arch with its great clock became in effect the front door to the campus when passengers disembarked at the station, which at that time was directly across the way, behind what today is the University Store. Blair and Stafford Little Halls were also a screen that hid the rest of the campus from the dirt and noise of the trains. The train and its tracks were an iron corset that hemmed in the western boundary of the campus. Once the tracks and station were relocated south in 1918, from opposite Blair to a site next to the present tennis courts, a considerable parcel of land was opened up. This made way for new dormitories to expand south and west rather than east, which had been an option, as shown at the beginning of the twentieth century by the construction 1879 Hall on Washington Road. A stroll up Blair Walk from Pyne Dormitory north toward Blair Tower, which parallels the former tracks, gives some idea of the land opened up to the university when the train station relocated.

Three decades before the land owned by the railroad became available for development on the western edge of the campus, the college purchased land that secured its boundary to the south. The acquisition of the 155-acre Potter Farm gave Princeton room to expand right up to the marshes through which flowed Stony Brook. Initially, those marshes offered little to the school beyond the legendary New Jersey mosquitoes and the occasional outbreak of disease. How the marsh was transformed into Princeton's greatest building project will be told at the last stop of this Walk.

The whole of the South Campus can be roughly divided into two triangular wedges. The first, defined by McCosh Walk on the north and Washington Road on the east, runs on a diagonal from McCormick Hall on the north down to Thomas Laboratory. As early as Cram's master plan of 1908, this precinct was zoned for academic purposes, including the new Graduate College, which would have been located approximately where McCosh Hall is today. The second and larger wedge to the west is filled primarily with dormitories and athletic facilities. This, too, conforms with the earliest master plans.

58. McCormick Art & Archeology

Ralph Adams Cram, 1922; Steinmann and Cain, 1966; Mitchell/Giurgola, 1989

Cram's choice of Venetian Gothic for the Department of Art and Archeology says a number of things about the high priest of the Collegiate Gothic style: it shows that Cram had more than one revivalist style in his quiver; it also shows that he was willing to defer to the other buildings in the area, Brown Hall in particular, and complement rather than challenge the neighborhood. It is not surprising that Cram would have chosen an Italianate style for a building dedicated to the study of art. But Venetian Gothic? What a stroke of wit! It is the sort of gesture only a supremely confident architect could have pulled off. The Venetian McCormick and its Florentine neighbor, Brown Hall, transplant the ancient artistic rivalry between Florence and Venice to the Princeton campus. In the history of art, neither city emerges as the clear winner, but at Princeton it is a brownstone and stucco Venice that dominates Florence to the south.

After Cram, succeeding generations of architects have added to, subtracted from, and in general pushed and pulled the building in all directions—beginning in 1927 when architects Sherley Morgan '13, Frederick D'Amato, and Francis Comstock '19 were commissioned to add a wing at the south end to accommodate classrooms, offices, and an exhibition room. The addition formed a closed court that was roofed over to provide space for modeling classes. Eight years later the architects Jean Labatut, Francis Comstock, and Eugene Batista renovated McCormick. They removed the roof of the court and added mosaics, which once decorated a third-century fountain in Antioch, a trophy of a Princeton archeological dig. In 1965 architects Steinmann, Cain, and White removed the earlier additions while at the same time enlarging and modernizing McCormick. Their intent was to make

McCormick Art & Archeology

Cram's original building an integral part of a larger project that included a new art museum. The modern elements of the somewhat ungainly structure that emerged are an exercise in curtain wall construction, featuring upended pinkish sandstone panels trimmed in travertine. These panels appear to be hung onto to a three-story horizontal slab whose windows run in continuous bands.

In 1989 the art complex was subjected to further surgery. The university dedicated a major addition to the Art Museum designed by the Philadelphia team of Mitchell/Giurgola, a firm whose work includes Australia's new parliament building in Canberra (1988). Short of reconstructing the entire complex, for which there was no budget, the architects seem to have had little choice but to defer to what was already there.

What can you say about a building that seems to have been assembled from pieces rather than designed? Like Frankenstein, the sutures are clearly visible. Not that the building is monstrous: the circulation routes of the public galleries work well enough; natural daylighting illuminates the galleries in a controlled way; and the quality of the museum's collection is memorable, certainly worth a trip to Princeton. Although Cram's original building is by no means the architect at his best, even tepid Cram has more visual interest than the modernist kudzu that wriggles around it. The Mitchell/Giurgola addition tries to take its cue from the older building, right down to the exterior colors and the red terra-cotta tiles on the pitched roof. But the modernist windows are simply punched holes in the facade that look all the more uninspired juxtaposed with the graceful way in which Cram handles a window. The back or south side is especially flat. It is one of

McCormick Art Museum

the few places on the Main Campus that might gain some visual interest by the addition of clever graffiti. Even Pablo Picasso's cast concrete, stone, and iron *Head of a Woman* (1971) at the front of the art museum fails to satisfy. It turns out not to have been executed by Picasso's own hand, but by the Norwegian artist Carl Nesjar. It is a Picasso all right, but whether it is art or a franchise may be open for debate.

Museum open: 10 am–5 pm, Tuesday–Saturday; 1 pm–5 pm, Sunday

59. School of Architecture

Fisher '23, Nes '28, Campbell, and Associates, 1963; interior remodeling, 1980

School of Architecture

A book should be written about the buildings in which America's 100-plus schools of architecture are housed. Considering this is where future generations of architects are trained, some chapters would make for unsettling reading. Princeton's entry to the list is a structure that wants you to like it, but it is a tough love. The Orange Key guide who led a small group, including the author, past the side that fronts McCosh Walk volunteered that it was her least favorite building on campus.

One of Princeton's three professional schools (Woodrow Wilson School of Public and International Affairs and the Engineering School being the other two), the School of Architecture was founded in 1919 and grew up on the other side of the Prospect garden in Cram's McCormick Hall. Designed and built around the same time as the Engineering Quad, the Architecture Building asserts a profoundly different intellectual agenda from its sister Art on the eastern edge of the campus. Initially at least, the similarities between the two appear obvious. No one would conclude that both were from any era other than the late 1950s and early 1960s—the rectilinear forms, the lack of ornament, the hard edges (as if honesty is angular and fiction curved), the flat roofs, the regular repetition of the windows lined up in such a way (directly over one another) to give the horizontal building some vertical thrust, the relative absence of wood to lend warmth and texture to the interiors (compare this to almost any building on campus designed after the 1980s), and the use of brick.

However, it is the way in which the designers of the Architecture School use brick that suggests how, despite a common aesthetic vocabulary, they are more successful than their engineering colleagues. Whereas one brick looks like the next at the E-Quad, the design team at the Architecture School specified brick that has been fired unevenly to create variations to the basic reddish-brown color. The effect is subtle but telling.

There are larger gestures, the most important of which is the attempt to break up the volumes to create a more human scale. In part this is dictated by the site, which infringes on the grounds of Prospect. The architects could not build too high, which would have been visually intrusive, nor could they go for long in any one direction horizontally, which would have created a wall. The result is two modest slabs set at right angles to one another to form a T, the stem of which is somewhat off center to the bar. The longer, east–west slab is three stories and complements the height of McCosh Hall, its neighbor to the north; the wing to the south is two stories in apparent deference to 1879 Hall to the east. The slabs are not directly connected, but are bridged by a narrow two-story hyphen or pavilion that serves as the entrance to both wings. The main stairs up to the library to the south and the design studios to the north are located here.

Unlike the E-Quad, the windows are not laid flush with the brick surface; instead, the brick steps out from the horizontal plane of the facade at regular intervals to form a series of two-story bays that project over a raised glass basement. This and the large recessed glass windows between the bays ought to give the building a welcome transparency. But this is not the case, since the glass appears to be coated from the inside with a film or membrane that makes it difficult to see in by day and out by night. In contrast to the clear glass and light gray limestone of McCosh Hall, the glass of the Architecture School looks gloomy. The use of such film to cut down the transference of radiant heat into or out of the glass curtain walls of the 1950s and 1960s was a common response to the worldwide energy crisis of the 1970s. The technology of so-called "low-emissivity glass" has since advanced beyond the undesirable color and light distortion of this earlier era. If and when the windows of the Architecture School are reglazed, the visual impact should be much improved and no doubt closer to the design the architects originally intended.

The repeated references to the Architecture School's neighbors are an important clue that suggests why this building looks better than the Engineering Quad even though they were built at the same time. The programs were different, to be sure. And, yes, there were more students studying the applied sciences. The E-Quad had to be larger. Yet these do not constitute sufficient reason for the numbing inertness of the complex on Olden Street. The Engineering Quad had no nearby university buildings to relate to and it was even too far east to benefit from the gravitational pull of Cram's master plan. Not so for the Architecture School. It was an infill building. The design team addressed constraints of site and surroundings, which shaped everything from the footprint of the building and the way the facade is manipulated (the bays) to the decision to use the materials familiar to this precinct of the campus—brick and limestone trim. The architects even use a horizontal band of stone (a string course) on the north–south wing to signal the division between the floors, just as on 1879 Hall.

When a recent graduate was asked to rate how the building worked, she gave it the equivalent of a B–. The windows admit plenty of natural light (a plus) and the openness of the design studio space facilitates an easy communication among students, which is another plus for this ideally collaborative art. She also noted the Architecture School was one of the few buildings on campus that offered passersby a view of students at work. On the negative side is the library, described as poorly laid out, too small, and gloomy in the stack areas. The faculty offices on the lower floor under the library were said to have the feel of a basement.

60. Woolworth Music Center

Moore and Hutchins, 1963; Juan Navarrow Baldeweg, renovation and addition, 1997

Woolworth Music Center

Throughout this guide, Princeton's architecture is often discussed by comparisons and contrasts. This has typically meant comparing one building to its neighbor or some other facility on campus. The Woolworth Music Center is an opportunity to apply the comparison–contrast approach to a single building, one with a dramatic, split personality.

When writing about the original building designed in 1963, it is almost too easy to dismiss it as a lumpish brick hat box set on top of a fieldstone shelf. Understandably the walls need to be thick to block the transfer of sound from either direction. But why does a building that is the home of music have to come off like a fortress with little if any pedestrian scale? From the outside it could as likely house the university's computer center as a chorus rehearsing Beethoven or a pianist playing Bach. From the inside, the hallways are claustrophobic. Worse than atonal, the building is tone deaf.

But then one looks slightly to the north to Baldeweg's so-called addition—talk about the tail wagging the dog. Inside and out, the other side of Woolworth is luminous. You have traveled from the equivalent of a 1960s black and white telecast to an MTV era that delights in blowing up the box into jagged pieces. Perhaps the most striking exterior details are two great light scoops that perch on the roof like an enormous metal-and-glass butterfly about to take flight. They bring light from the north and south into the depths of the building. By thrusting up and out from the flat plane of the roof, the scoops return visual interest to a part of a building that for many modernists was simply a way to keep out the rain—something flat roofs do not always do so well.

True, the eastern elevation of Baldeweg's addition is hardly pedestrian friendly. It is a brick wall, although the brick is a livelier hue of red than that used on the older half of the building on the left. But once you walk inside the east entrance hyphen, which ties the two personalities of Woolworth together, one discovers a glass clerestory and roof on the right side that diffuses daylight into the below-grade McAlpin Rehearsal Hall. The trapezoidal rehearsal hall may be subterranean, but the architect orchestrates the space to be a well of light. Indeed, throughout the heart of the addition, which is a floor-to-ceiling atrium, the use of daylighting and material is bracing without being over-wrought. The atrium is paved with the same brick as the outside stairs and terrace. This is just one of the design strategies to break down the boundaries between inside and out. Directly in front, and the focal point of the atrium, is the rounded clear-glass wall of the three-story Sheide Music Library (Class of '36), which noses into the space like the prow of a sleek boat revealing all the passengers inside—students doing their research. The third material besides the glass and brick is the blonde wood of the entrance and the library floor. Straight ahead to the west there is a view of Prospect garden. Above this west entrance there stretches a bright Kelly green metal louvered awning that runs along the back. Against the red brick the awning looks like a blank musical staff awaiting notes.

Back inside the spacious atrium, the visual interest of the music library is echoed on the other side by flights of stairs that appear to be carved out of the wall. Where railings are required for reasons of safety, the architect uses waist-high glass, creating balcony-like spaces that look into the atrium. These and other gestures result in a great interior room that celebrates geometry and light as voices tune, violins ride up and down strings, and a pianist bangs out scales. In short, the distance between the split personality of Woolworth Hall is the distance between a mere facility and architecture.

61. 1879 Hall   *Benjamin W. Morris, 1904*

1879 Hall

This formerly residential facility, built early in the twentieth century, is evidence of the direction in which the campus might have grown if the trustees had not been able shortly thereafter to secure large parcels of land to the south. Afterwards, no other dormitory was built this far east. A handsome brick exercise in Tudor Gothic, 1879 Hall was hugely popular with Princeton's upperclassmen for the very reason that it was the closest student residence to the Prospect Avenue Eating Clubs. Just how hand-

1879 Hall

some it appeared to the collective eyes of students can be gathered from a contemporary handbook: "The suites consist of a study, in which is set an open fireplace, and two single bedrooms, separated from the study by a passage opening from the stair hall." The building's use for residential life ended in 1960, when the university converted it to administrative offices. The conversion is a reminder of the continuing authority of Cram's 1907 masterplan, which identified this precinct as an academic rather than a residential zone.

When Wilson was president of Princeton, he had his room over the vaulted archway, a privilege no doubt earned by the fact he was a member of the class that had donated the dormitory. This room has its own special entrance, an impressive limestone and brick open stone stairway along the inside of the northeast corner of the arch. In designing the passageway through the center of 1879 Hall, Morris (1870–1944) was not simply interested in traffic control; he seized the opportunity to engage in visual choreography. Like a telescope, the arch is placed just so that it focuses the eye, leading the line of sight forward and out to a vista down Prospect or a great outdoor room if approached from the east. The progression from light to shadow back to light is a source of theater, a script that is reversed at night, but with the same effect: there is a dramatic sense of entering and departing.

1879 Hall

All this seems obvious until one compares it to what happens when an architect either has no interest in or knowledge of similar effects. Go to the passageway leading into the garden at the center of the Engineering Quad: there is no vista, no choreography, nothing to draw one in.

Collegiate Gothic archways are like rooms, decorated rooms. Look up: a lamp sways slightly in the breeze; the ribs of the triple-groined vaults give texture; the bosses or limestone ornaments that pin the intersecting ribs of each groin are carved with oak leaves or the heads of snarling tigers. There is a personality, a spirit to the place. Students often gather here to sing. (Its hard to imagine anyone would stop in the passageway that tunnels through McCormick to sing *Old Nassau*)

Before moving on, the arch at 1879 Hall deserves one more comment, because it is a reminder that doorways and arches often serve as frames for the vistas on the other side as much as for the people passing through. The reader is as likely at this point in the book to have taken a picture of a friend or had a picture of oneself taken just outside and at the center of one of Princeton's many Collegiate Gothic arches. If not, 1879 Hall provides a particularly handsome frame with its limestone quoins, monkeys and tigers, and flanking octagonal brick towers.

Looking first at the east and then the west face of the arch, compare how the architect subtly varies the height of the flanking towers and the placement of windows as well as the gargoyles (sculpted by Gutzon Borglum (1871–1941), who would later turn his hand to the presidential faces on Mount Rushmore). Which is the higher tower on the east face? Which on the west? How does the placement of the windows and gargoyles differ on both elevations? What is achieved by the variety? For that matter, what is achieved by the elaborate copper box-like heads or "leaders" that carry rainwater to the downspouts? Ornament requires not only greater cost during the initial construction, but also a greater investment in upkeep and maintenance. Some of those limestone gargoyles are clearly disintegrating. Is it worth the cost? Sooner or later architecture that is not simply functional makes us confront this question. What is the purpose of ornament?

> Allow not nature more than nature needs,
> Man's life is cheap as beast's.
> —William Shakespeare, *King Lear*, Act II, scene ii

Guyot Hall

62. Guyot Hall   *William Berryman Scott; Parrish and Schroeder, 1909*

Guyot Hall was the last academic building that went up during Woodrow Wilson's presidency. Its construction fulfilled a commitment made years earlier by President McCosh to invest in Princeton's outstanding reputation in the sciences. Nineteenth-century geniuses such as Joseph Henry (research physicist) and Arnold Henry Guyot (geology) worked in primitive facilities. In that regard, Princeton was no better or worse than other colleges. But by the middle of the nineteenth century, new scientific and technical schools provided modern accommodations for technical education. Even older institutions such as Harvard were building state-of-the-art facilities. If succeeding generations of outstanding talent were to be attracted to Princeton, first-rate labs, classrooms, and offices for faculty and students alike had to be a priority.

Building and designing them, however, were not the same thing. Architects were challenged by their clients to chart new territory, since there was little precedent. After all, the pursuit of the theoretical and applied sciences is a kind of education radically different from the traditional classical curriculum, which favored rhetoric, religion, and philosophy. A curriculum grounded in experimentation and close observation of the physical world demanded a new way of building—for example, the ability to quickly vent foul-smelling and perhaps even deadly gases from a chemistry lab. Long before the twentieth century, Princeton's Joseph Henry grasped this when he said in a speech to his colleagues that the architecture of science "should be looked upon more as a useful than a fine art....In building, we should plan the inside first, and then plan the outside to cover it." In other words, his ideal was an architecture that would be practical, flexible, and, to use a term from our own day, wired.

Guyot Hall gargoyle

Guyot, Palmer Hall to the north, and indeed the laboratories and classrooms to the south—Moffett, Schultz, and Thomas—are best understood as decorated sheds. Their *beauty*, to those who use them, is primarily a function of their utility. But what about those of us who aren't working inside? How should such architecture talk to us? Over the years, this challenge has been met in three ways, all of which are visible from Guyot: decorate the exterior so that it fits in with the rest of the campus (Palmer and Guyot); present a clean, no-nonsense face that equates scientific truth with objectivity and makes a clear break with the past (Moffett); or try to invent a design vocabulary that while straightforward, nevertheless is allusive and poetic (Schultz and Thomas Laboratories). The latter could be said to be the architectural equivalent of writing blank verse.

Guyot Hall is literally a fraction of what it was supposed to be. The architects had intended a large quadrangle whose dimensions would have been 288 feet by 256 feet. In fact, only the north wing was built, a four-story structure 288 feet long and 60 feet deep, which yielded nearly two acres of laboratory, class, office, and exhibition space. Functionally, the building was programmed in two parts: biology to the east; geology in the west. Both programs are announced on the exterior by a wonderful parade of carved limestone gargoyles, 200 in all: living species are represented on the biology wing to the east; extinct species are on the geology wing to the west. This arrangement first appeared in England's history museums, which became the model for Princeton. Field glasses are recommended, since the animals cavort high up at the roof line. It is a welcome touch of whimsy to a structure that with its dark brick, flat roof, squared-off symmetrical towers, buttresses, and sheer size conveys massiveness rather than majesty.

The two crenellated towers at the front or north side identify the main pedestrian entrances and internal stairways. The companion towers at the rear are elevator shafts. The Natural History Museum, which was established in 1875 by Professor Guyot in the Prayer Room of Nassau Hall, was moved to the first floor, where it is located today, although no longer taking up the entire ground floor. Given the rapid progress of scientific investigation in the twentieth century, it is not surprising that Guyot has witnessed a number of extensive interior renovations, such as the Geosciences Library (Mitchell/Giurgola, 1981), as well as several substantial additions, including the George M. Moffett Biological Laboratory (O'Connor and Kilham, 1960), along the west side of Washington Road, and the Schultz Laboratory to the south. With these additions, the size of Guyot Hall today closely approximates the ambitious plans of its original architects.

63. Thomas Molecular Laboratory and George LaVie Schultz Laboratory

Robert Venturi '47, exterior; Payette and Associates, interior laboratories; 1986

The last two buildings on this walk are considered part of a single vision, programmatically and aesthetically. The Thomas Molecular (1986) and George LaVie Schultz Laboratories (1993) are the products of the same design team—Payette and Associates, specialists in laboratory design for the interiors, and Robert Venturi '47 for the outside. Both facilities represent a major commitment by the university in the 1980s to establish an international presence in molecular biology.

The first built, the four-story, 110,000-square-foot Thomas Laboratory, honors the eminent molecular biologist and author, Lewis Thomas '33. Here is a building that wears its program on its sleeve. The scale, rhythm, and proportion of the facades are determined by the specific requirements of program and interior layout. The two long elevations are characterized for the first three floors by a consistent rhythm of identical window bays that echo the rhythm of the lab–office modules inside. The top floor, which houses the mechanical plant, is wrapped in a recessive brick and cast stone pattern. On either end of the building are lounges fronted by large bay windows that look out to the campus. The lounges are not the only gesture toward encouraging human interaction in what might otherwise be an impersonal laboratory space: The corridors are wide, ceilings are relatively high, and glass walls between the labs and internal support spaces bring in natural light and afford views across the building's width.

Thomas Laboratory

The wide corridors also allow for the storage of equipment when necessary. If light and transparency are gestures that humanize the environment, the architects underscore their intent by a liberal use of oak on wall rails, doors, furniture, and casework. The non-load-bearing internal partitions can be reconfigured easily to accommodate the evolving needs of a science that relatively speaking is still in its infancy.

Venturi, who popularized the concept of the "decorated shed," applies his art to give variety to what might otherwise be a long, inert rectangle. The bays at either end and the handling of the mechanical plant on the top floor have already been cited. Most of the other design strategies on the exterior are decorative, focusing on color and patterns in the brickwork and cast stone. But where there is a practical reason, Venturi is prepared to go beyond decoration. For example, the windows on the south side are recessed to reduce the heat and glare of the sun. This also helps mitigate some of the flatness of the long south elevation. In what appears to be a witty allusion to Princeton's long tradition of Collegiate Gothic architecture, the main north entrance is topped by a somewhat flattened ogee arch. In a building whose surface decoration is dominated by rectangles, squares, and diamonds, this unexpected sinuous line over the front door is a welcome surprise. It also draws the eye to the portal through which one gains entry into the building. The project so impressed the architectural community that it received a national AIA Honor Award in 1987.

Seven years later the same team designed Schultz Laboratory, named for its principal donor, George LaVie Schultz '40. Schultz stands just across the way and helps define the north edge of Goheen Walk, a major east/west pedestrian axis that runs across this sector of the campus from the train station to the stadium. As is the case with Thomas Laboratory, color and pattern are the main design resources used to break up the mass of the basically rectangular addition to Moffett Hall. The brick that runs under and above the rows of paired windows on the south entry facade is interrupted by the cast stone between the windows. The stone casing on either side of the windows imparts texture and a bit of vertical lift. The dominant material on the exterior of the first floor and around the entrance is likewise stone and invokes the traditional brick and limestone pattern indigenous to this area of the campus.

Venturi has a field day paying homage to the Collegiate Gothic architecture familiar to him from his years as a Princeton undergraduate and graduate student. The use, for example, of green slate for the walkways into the lobby and the floor of the lobby itself is a fond echo of the older tradition. The single large limestone column, which is cut into the facade at the entrance, revives the importance of ceremonious front doors. The gray granite band that runs just below the top of the column suggests a classical capital. The fact that the entrance is tucked under the second story recalls the porches of Collegiate Gothic as well as Victorian buildings. Setting the entry door at an oblique angle allows the porch to have more depth than would otherwise be possible on a tight site. The manner in which the entrance is designed also allows for the play of light and shadow, day and night. The window glass is not a single light, but divided into panes, suggesting leaded mullions. The one-and-a-half story glass entry bays render the lower story transparent, allowing the eye to travel easily inside, where the hallway and wainscoted offices run along the front edge.

The massing of the building follows a classical order of base, shaft, and capital, the latter of which is somewhat top-heavy. The west elevation expands on a number of the decorative elements used on the front. Like the front, there are clear visual clues that distinguish the bottom from the top, the most obvious of which are the windows on the southwest corner. These graduate from the largest, on the ground floor, to the smallest at the top or fifth story. In place of the cast stone on the front, the lower story on this side is yellow brick; above the brick, the surface appears to be gypsum board with large brown squares stenciled on the surface, echoing the checker-board squares on the west upper story of Thomas Laboratory across the way. Approaching the two laboratories from the west, one immediately sees that the relationship between the buildings is flagged by the squares. Yet on Schultz, the effect is curiously low-rent the closer one approaches. It appears to be the architectural equivalent of a sheet of canvas draped over a work in progress. Indeed, the entire south campus is a work in progress.

George LaVie Schultz Laboratory

South Campus

The path of development in this quadrant of the south campus may be understood largely as a response to the railroad that runs at its western edge. But that is not the whole story. The other key player was Princeton's first supervising architect, Ralph Adams Cram. It was Cram's 1908 masterplan that zoned the land for residential purposes. This walk of twentieth-century campus housing begins with a couple of representative examples of the earliest Collegiate Gothic style, then continues through various attempts—some more successful than others—to discover an authentic contemporary voice, briefly visiting two residential colleges, and ends with a view of one of Princeton's greatest building projects, Lake Carnegie.

64. Cuyler Hall   *Day Brothers and Klauder, 1912*

Tagged by almost every commentator as the most handsome of Princeton's residential halls, Cuyler Hall is Collegiate Gothic at its most inventive. There is a richness of detail and materials, from the over-scaled stone chimneys and thick, almost fudge-like slabs of slate on the roof, to the extravagant ceiling of the Pitney archway (installed in 1921), which honors the long relationship between the Pitney family and Princeton. If a spider could spin stone webs, the ceiling inside Pitney archway would be the result with rosettes, leaves, coats of arms, and shields caught like so many flies on the sticky web. The fact that the L-shaped Cuyler is Princeton's smallest dormitory makes it seem a privileged place. Designed and constructed at the same time as the great steel plates of the Titanic were being riveted together, Cuyler looks back to an era of handcraftsmanship—and that is the point.

It is no accident that the passion for Collegiate Gothic comes at the moment when the Industrial Revolution was transforming American culture, and even the pace and perception of time itself. However, like any revolution, it was bound to provoke a reaction. Just as Princeton's founders had deliberately chosen a site for the college away from the ostensible folly of the nation's young cities, a century-and-a-half later such men as univer-

Cuyler Hall

Pitney arch, Cuyler Hall

sity President Wilson and Princeton's trustees mandated a style of architecture that intellectually and aesthetically represented an idyllic alternative to the sweat, grime, and, yes, ethnicity of the great industrial cities of the late-nineteenth and early-twentieth centuries.

If Princeton's graduates were to be "in the Nation's service," to use Wilson's phrase, they must be cultivated to be high-minded gentlemen. This required a carefully choreographed, well-bred environment. Instead of smokestacks, there would be Culyer's chimneys and fireplaces; instead of mass-produced construction, there would be the patient craftsmanship of Pitney archway. If this required transplanting entire communities of English, Irish, and Italian stonemasons and woodworkers to produce the desired effect, Princeton was prepared to book their passage.

In short, the choice of the Collegiate Gothic style for Cuyler Hall and throughout Princeton at this point of the school's history was not a simple aesthetic preference in the way you might pick a blue tie over a yellow one; it was a style that carried profound ideological freight, the meaning of which was first articulated sixty years before by the influential English writer and critic John Ruskin (1819–1900). Here is Ruskin, from *Works*, volume ten, on the rise of mass production and the division of labor:

> Wherever the workman is utterly enslaved, the parts of the building must of course be absolutely like each other; for the perfection of his execution can only be reached by exercising him in doing one thing, and giving him nothing else to do. The degree in which the workman is degraded may be thus known at a glance, by observing whether the several parts of the building are similar or not....if, as in Gothic work, there is perpetual change both in design and execution: the workman must have been altogether set free.

No wonder it was so difficult to abandon Collegiate Gothic a half century later. Yet, in spite of Ruskin's powerful ideological message, there was a growing conviction that as the century progressed architecture should look pure, sleek, and machine-made.

65. Dillon Gymnasium *Aymar Embury '00, 1947*

Immediately to the west of Culyer Hall, across Elm Drive, stands the crenellated towers of Dillon Gym. Along with Firestone Library, it has the distinction of being among the last structures on campus built in the Collegiate Gothic style. Dillon Gymnasium (named for Herbert Lowell Dillon '07, its principal donor) was the third of a series of evermore large athletic facilities that began with Bonner in 1869, the first gymnasium of any American college. Next came Cope and Stewardson's University Gymnasium, which, when it opened in 1903, was the largest gym in the country. While similar in

Dillon Gymnasium

many of its exterior details, the building we see today is not University Gym, which was destroyed by fire in 1944. Dillon is the phoenix that rose three years later out of the ashes.

Although a gymnasium is basically little more than a large shed that spans a great, largely open space, a college gym can inspire an almost religious-like affection in those who have spent time within its walls, as either players or spectators. It is not an overstatement to say that Cope and Stewardson's Gymnasium was a shrine right down to the Trophy Room, the holiest of holy spaces. When it was destroyed, trophies and all, Princeton demanded the new gymnasium be built in the same spot and virtually recreate the look of its predecessor. Firestone Library was to have been Princeton's great bicentennial project, but it was Dillon Gymnasium that took that honor.

For all its similarities, from the use of local stone (Lockatong argillite) with limestone trim (salvaged from the older building) to the great crenellated entry tower, Embury's design is not a slavish replication. For one thing, Princeton's growth over the years and the flood of returning veterans necessitated a larger facility. The main interior space of the older gymnasium was 100 by 106 feet. Dillon measured 210 by 100 feet. The greater size accommodated a state-of-the-art swimming facility, which was built in a one-story wing on the south side. As for the tower, which like its predecessor echoes the tower with its four octagonal turrets over Blair Arch (also by Cope and Stewardson), Embury moved it from the north, where it had stood in the old gymnasium, to the east side. It was a sensible move. On the north, short wall, the tower would have sat like a cork in the neck of a bottle. Also sensible in an era before air conditioning are the large operable windows, which let in light and air to the deep interior spaces.

Embury dressed Dillon with carved gargoyles, the last building on campus that animated its walls with a full program of these wonderful stone creatures. Compare this to Firestone Library, where the few grotesques are applied half-heartedly to the surface. On Dillon, the cartoon-like athletes carved in stone still show some of the same playfulness that never fails to delight.

66. Pyne Hall *Day and Klauder, 1922*

The architecture of Pyne Hall is of less historic interest than the forces that shaped it. For one, it was the first building to use the land made available by the relocation in 1918 of the train station and tracks. In addition, its siting in relation to the overall campus was significant. In effect, it is the second of two bookends, the first being Holder Hall. Just as Holder Quad defines the northwest corner of the campus, the open-ended Pyne Quad, which faces the north, was meant in its day to define and anchor the southwest.

Pyne was also the first dormitory built after the First World War, which undoubtedly explains its large size—one of the largest dorms on campus, in fact, with 177 rooms. As early as 1908, the campus architect, Ralph Adams Cram, had earmarked this quadrant for dormitories in response to the university's pressing need for student housing. It had long been an article of faith that to develop a community of gentleman scholars, Princeton must be a residential school. The cessation of all building at the outbreak of the World War I and then, after the Armistice, the flood of returning veterans made matters desperate. In 1920 a quarter of the students lived in off-campus rooming houses. The university had to build big— and fast. Yet even as late as 1921 when construction of Pyne began, materials were still somewhat scarce because of the war. As a consequence of this scarcity and the fast track construction, Pyne Hall, not surprisingly, is built in a much plainer and less ornamented style than a pre-war building such as Cuyler or the dormitories that followed.

Finding the funds to build this and the other dormitories that soon followed—Henry and Foulke (both 1923)—also presented the university with a challenge. But here death, both natural and that caused by the war, proved to be an unanticipated source of funds. In April 1921, one of Princeton's greatest benefactors died, Moses Taylor Pyne, the man who in his position as chairman of the Grounds and Buildings Committee persuaded the trustees to adopt Collegiate Gothic as the school's official style. It was pre-ordained that Princeton's alumni would generously underwrite a major project that would honor his memory. Funding opportunities offered themselves thanks to the fact that Princeton's Collegiate Gothic dormitories feature separate entries rather than long double loaded corridors. These individual entries are today designated as gifts of the Classes of 1902, 1906, 1908, 1912, 1920, 1921, 1922, and 1923. Nearly fifty years after it was dedicated, Pyne became the first dormitory to house undergraduate women.

67. Spelman Halls *I. M. Pei, 1973*

"Given in memory of Laura Spelman Rockefeller by her grandson Laurance Spelman Rockefeller '32 and dedicated to her belief in equality and opportunity." A half century later and about fifty yards to the south of Pyne Hall, the Collegiate Gothic affection for axial compositions and rational planning reaches an unexpected apotheosis in the work the renowned modernist, I. M. Pei (1907–), did for Princeton. Pei juggles the familiar vocabulary of Princeton's quadrangles, removes one side, pulls together what remains, and

Spelman Halls

comes up with two sets of triangles. It is a geometric figure that has fascinated Pei most of his creative life, the East Building of Washington's National Gallery and the glass pyramid outside the Louvre being two familiar examples.

The triangle is one of the smallest musical instruments in an orchestra, but in Pei's hands, the triangle makes a mighty sound. A student of the Hungarian modernist Marcel Breuer (1902–1981), Pei took to heart the lessons of his master's uncompromising structural purity, including the use of flat roofs. Constructed of modern materials, including great expanses of glass, one building is pretty much like the next. Variety is achieved not by any change to the shape, but by rotating the eight dormitories of the complex in tic-toc fashion, on pre-existing pedestrian paths that intersect to form another set of triangles. It is easy to imagine the architect working out his concept with the basic tools of lined graph paper and a straight-edge.

In explaining what he wanted his design for these residences to achieve, Pei laid out three objectives: one, to continue the campus' traditional sequence of open space, building enclosure, and vista; (2) to preserve openness and existing landscape; and (3) to promote informal student meetings and a community spirit without sacrificing privacy. His objectives represent an insightful description of how the Princeton campus actually works. On the first two counts, Pei clearly succeeds. But one is left to wonder about the third.

Each of the 58 apartments is a complete domestic unit with living and dining areas, outside balcony, full kitchen, bath, and four private study bedrooms. The entry stairway, which is open to the full height of the building and sky-lit, relates the house unit to the path that runs by and forms the dominant architectural element around which each building is organized. Here again, Pei is responding to the older tradition of Collegiate Gothic residential design. He gives us an updated version of the Princeton entry form of housing as opposed to long corridors. However, acknowledging an older tradition is one thing; both in form and function, the shape of the buildings signals that a corner has been turned—a precise, hard-edged corner. If the Collegiate Gothic architect took pains to give the illusion if not the reality of hand-wrought materials, Pei leaves no doubt that what we see is 979 precast floor and wall panels weighing up to 38,000 pounds—shop fabricated and field assembled.

How well does it work in practice? That depends on one's perspective. There is no question that contemporary construction techniques yield certain savings. Here, construction time was cut in half—from 24 to 13 months. Also, the geometric sculpturesque forms are undeniably arresting amid the organic ebb and flow of the surrounding landscape. The impact is amplified by the fact that the hard-edged geometry is robed in the favorite color of modernists—white. But walking in, around, and under the buildings, this author found the pedestrian level arresting but also vaguely alienating. Nevertheless, by consciously working within Princeton's older design tradition, Pei opened a door that the architect Robert Venturi would walk through a decade later.

68. New Quad, 1937 Dormitory (Wilson College)

Sherwood, Mills, and Smith, 1960

On the walk between Spelman Halls and Wilson College, you pass the tennis courts and the Tennis Pavilion designed by Ballard, Todd, and Snibbs, which received an AIA Honor Award in 1962. East of the tennis courts stands Wilson College. Founded in 1968, Woodrow Wilson College is the oldest of the five residential colleges and houses approximately 500 students. It includes a dining hall and seven dormitories, most of which were designed by the modernist firm of Sherwood, Mills, and Smith.

Smith, who was an alumnus (1930), and his firm tried to pull off what was perhaps impossible: find a style other than Collegiate Gothic for the first residential-dining hall complex the university had built in more than forty years. The manner was to be new, but not too new; modern, but not too modern. Consistent with this precinct, the construction would be brick with limestone trim around the windows. In plan, the scheme for what came to be called the "New Quad" seems to owe something to Mies van der Rohe's 1940 masterplan for the Illinois Institute of Technology (IIT) campus, right down to the repetitive rectangular slabs, complete with the flat roofs but minus the Miesian exposed steel-frame structural system. The IIT scheme had been widely published and hailed as the first truly modern campus design. With that kind of press, it would have been hard not to have read from the Mies book, although whether because of the sloping terrain or the presence of existing buildings, the architects arranged the buildings in a more relaxed, open quadrangle.

Unfortunately for the architects and Princeton, the six buildings of the New Quad look a lot like Jersey motel modern. One half expects to see a neon sign on the roof and soda and ice machines against the pale, drab brick. Visually, the New Quad presented a dispirited advertisement for the inauguration of Princeton's first residential college, a concept President Wilson had attempted to launch (unsuccessfully) a half century earlier. Obviously the concept of residential colleges had a greater attraction than the package in which it first arrived. It did not hurt that the New Quad offered the first dining hall conveniently located on the south side of the campus. Whatever the reason, the Wilson experiment took root and paved the way for the system of residential colleges as a way of life for Princeton's freshmen and sophomores. In the years since its dedication, nature and Princeton's deservedly famous landscaping have softened the raw edges of the New Quad and it has receded into the shrubs and trees. A little ivy can do wonders.

69. Clapp Hall and Feinberg Hall (Wilson College)

Clapp Hall   *Koetter, Kim, and Associates, 1987*
Feinberg Hall   *Tod Williams '65 and Associates, 1986*

Feinberg Hall

But this is not the last word on Wilson College. Clapp and Feinberg jolt us back into the world of the vertical. Both starkly define as well as stand apart from the Cold War infatuation the rest of New Quad has with repetition, parallel lines, and right angles. In his description of Feinberg, the architect refers to spirals (the interior stairs) and *mystery*—"the dark tower."

Towers, steeply-pitched gable roofs, light, and shadow—a Gothic if not Victorian sensibility animates how the architect uses his materials to create a building that, like Holder and Blair towers, is a directional finder. By constricting the pedestrian passage from the upper campus down into the Wilson College court, Feinberg reinterprets in strictly contemporary imagery the movement through a Collegiate Gothic archway, from one outdoor room to the next. There is the ceremonial experience of entry and exit. The architect has given Wilson College a front door.

If the early 1960s architecture conveys a modernist message of mechanical repetition and minimalism, Feinberg, in both form and plan, broadcasts a commitment to diversity and deconstructivism. On floors two through four, rooms are arranged into six suites that house four students each. On the first floor, a special four-person suite can be used by physically disabled students. The top, fifth floor, has two six-person suites, each a duplex with upstairs-downstairs spaces. All the suites afford distinct views of the campus, which perhaps is why students have dubbed Feinberg the "Fishbowl." Fishbowl or not, the architect offers the residents a surprise. He has reinterpreted the Collegiate Gothic affection for the separate entries, rather than the modernist love for long corridors. But instead of arranging these entries horizontally, they are stacked one on top of another.

Eighty feet tall, the 40-by-40-foot building features brick- and block-bearing wall construction with wooden floors on concrete planking. On every side, there is an aggressive pursuit of texture. For instance, the brick is overscaled, Norman size and the color is a rich plum or aubergine with iron spotting. The joints are raked horizontally to help give a basically vertical building a sense of weight. Windows are steel and glass and the steeply-inclined roof is a steel frame clad in standing-seam copper. There is no illusion here of craftsmen patiently plying their art. Yet it is also clear that in the hands of a creative architect, mass-produced materials can be made to yield art.

Two stair towers reinforce the perpendicular. The prefabricated interior stair system with its green Vermont slate treads spirals around a narrow shaft of space connecting the ground floor to a skylight 80 feet above. The exterior north stair is a small tower unto itself, encircling an elevator shaft and topped by an inverted steel and wire glass canopy, which parodies the steeply pitched roof. The tower is tied back to the building at the landings. It provides an alternate circulation path as well as back porches to the student suites. The effect interests the eye, accommodates the social needs of the occupants, and imaginatively fulfills the requirements of the state fire codes. In 1988 Feinburg Hall received an AIA Honor Award for design excellence.

70. Lourie-Love Hall (Butler College)

Hugh Stubbins and Associates, 1964

Lourie-Love Hall

With the full force of the Boomer generation about to hit the campus in the 1960s, Princeton commissioned a second complex of five dormitories just south of the New Quad on what had been playing fields. Of course this was immediately christened the "New New Quad," until it became the nucleus of Butler College, Princeton's second residential complex.

By comparing the footprint of the two neighboring quads, one immediately sees the different design strategy taken by Stubbins and Associates. The architect of Lourie-Love Hall was less reluctant to draw from the Collegiate Gothic well. As Stubbins wrote at the time, his intent was "to capture the traditional scale [of Collegiate Gothic] in a modern idiom." What Stubbins had in mind was nothing so superficial as a perfunctory bow to brick and limestone trim—although he does not shy away from that gesture—but rather a more profound understanding of concepts that go beyond the matter of mere surface detail. For instance, instead of the unrelieved flat planes of the New Quad rectangles, Stubbins suggests Gothic bays by staggering the wall planes. If New Quad is inert, New New Quad shimmies. Although there are no towers per se, the heights of the buildings vary. A sense of the vertical is further reinforced by thin projecting planes that are perpendicular to the facade. This, Stubbins says, is his take on buttresses.

There is more. Even though the roof of Lourie-Love Hall, as well as the others in the quad, is as flat as its neighbors in the New Quad, Stubbins wanted to introduce some action. So he places a decorative metal fence or parapet along the edge. He intended these to suggest Gothic crenellations. But the effort was forced and almost from the beginning became the butt of many jokes: "Why are those bicycle racks up on the roof?" Less arbitrary was the way Stubbins sited Lourie-Love and the rest of the buildings in the complex. He pulled them closer together to create two modest courts. By doing so, he reinterpreted in modern terms the cherished sequence of open space and enclosure that works so well throughout the older precincts of the campus. The impact of these spaces is further enhanced by attractive landscaping. The Class of 1941 Court between Lourie-Love and 1941 Dormitory breaks up what would otherwise be a monotonous space by dividing it into several levels, which are reached by low stone steps. Every April the entire area is canopied under pink saucers of magnolia blossoms. These and other plantings soften the relentless straight lines of the modernist idiom.

On balance, then, while perhaps not worth a voyage across the Atlantic, Lourie-Love and its companions in the New New Quad are agreeable in a way that eluded the architects just up the hill.

71. Gordon Wu Hall (Butler College) *Robert Venturi '47, 1983*

The lesson of a design like Feinberg Hall is clear: a single building can impart a sense of place to an otherwise amorphous setting. The modern master who showed the way was a gifted alumnus. Robert Venturi, like many of his contemporaries, was disturbed by what he saw as a drastic drop in the quality of Princeton's architecture since the glory days of Collegiate Gothic. Unlike many of his contemporaries, Venturi did something about it.

Like Wilson College, the new Butler College (1980) was a collection of buildings in search of a focus. Consider Patton Hall (1906), with its Gothic turrets and leaded windows, in awkward company with the modernist complex of townhouse dorms designed by Hugh Stubbins, which in turn is a neighbor of Aymar Embury's 1915 Hall (1949), described by architecture critic Paul Goldberger as a "timid mix of Georgian and Tudor."

How to make this all hang together, and provide a dining hall cum social facility for the new college? Venturi's solution was, in his words, "to create something like Holder Court, but less explicit." In the short run, he succeeded in refereeing the architectural equivalent of a sprawling Charles Ives symphony. But there was a more lasting impact: Venturi demonstrated that a modern architect did not have to turn his back on history. His reference to Holder Court is not a throwaway line. The best way to understand Venturi's achievement is to hike back to Holder Court, take a look at the Commons, and then return to Wu Hall and look through the window into the dining hall. The echoes are unmistakable: a modern interpretation of a great Gothic dining hall right down to the chandeliers.

His starting point was Wilcox, the existing dining hall of Wilson College. Located at the southwest edge of the New Quad, Wilcox could become the hinge around which both colleges turned. Space, though tight, was available, since the land immediately to the west of Wilcox was occupied by loading docks and dumpsters. Thinking of that indefinite, under-utilized space between Wilson and Butler Colleges as a lock, Venturi made Wu Hall work like a key. By an act of creative legerdemain, Venturi slid the key into place and opened up a precinct of delight.

Wu Hall introduces many of the strategies Venturi would use in his later designs for Princeton—applied surface decoration, rounded bays, bands of mullioned windows set against a brick facade, brick patterns that suggest belt courses and friezes, horizontal lines, a liberal use of interior woods, transparent interior spaces—looking in and seeing out—and ceremonial entrances. This is not meant to suggest Venturi is repetitious because his architecture has a characteristic look. It means his designs are as individual and idiosyncratic as a thumbprint or signature.

But how does the architecture work? The grand oak stairway north of the entry hall functions as an armature around which turn the opposing rhythms of relaxation (you can sit and watch the world go by) and motion (these are stairs). The one element that perhaps shows most persuasively why critics rank Wu as one of the best buildings on campus is the front west facade that defines the eastern edge of Butler Walk. The tight site dictated that Wu Hall would be long and narrow. Venturi had to break up a flat surface to ensure that one's experience with the building would be more than an encounter with a wall. Venturi interrupts horizontal and vertical members: the ground floor is a curtain wall with a procession of white, over-scaled, and nonfunctional keystones; immediately inside are free-standing white columns; one flight up, the plane of the upper stories is broken by deep recesses (which relate to the massing of the second floor of 1915 Hall across the way); the roof line is also broken up to suggest what has been called a "skyline"; the eyebrow window near the south end creates a pause; the same effect is created by the gray granite and white marble pattern above the entrance; and then, of course, there are the bays on either end. What may initially seem arbitrary surface detail is in fact carefully calculated to suggest a texture and complexity that transforms a blank wall into a lively facade.

Wu Hall

Venturi has access to such gestures because he is not afraid of tradition; nor his he afraid of taking risks. Like Princeton's Victorian and Collegiate Gothic architects, he has the confidence to be eclectic without giving up his standing as a modern architect. His mullions may suggest Gothic leaded windows, but there is no doubt they are manufactured, not hand-crafted. Wu Hall is a pivotal building in Princeton's architectural history: it marked the end of an era in which Princeton's architects struggled to define themselves against their legacy and opened the way to future achievement. Venturi's achievement earned an AIA National Honor Award in 1984.

Before moving on, take one final look at the entryway: the curiously elaborate decorative elements, dating back to Elizabethan and Jacobean precedents, present the best in contemporary zoomorphism—the pointed ears (those obelisks), the eyes (those ovals), the nose and whiskers by the doors. It is a feline turn by an artist at the top of his game.

72. Scully Dormitories *Michado and Silvetti, 1998*

The wind that blows from the southeast carries the murmur of commuter traffic from U.S. Route 1. Against this stands the massive, three connected wings of Princeton's newest dormitories. Of the three, the south wing is clearly intended to be the focus. With its stern, square tower and saw-toothed gables faced in slate, this side of Scully suggests a sort of Maginot Line. Above and behind these penthouse gables are angular skylights that look like observation posts for the troops inside. The great one-and-a-half square archway that leads south from the quadrangle out to the open grassy fields could just as easily house a portcullis poised to slam shut should New Jersey's suburban subdivisions and strip malls ever threaten to cross Lake Carnegie. If Holder is the university's redoubt on Nassau Street, Scully secures the southern flank—almost. There is still an opening on the southwest that leaves half of Butler College exposed. Not surprisingly the university has plans to build another dormitory to plug up the gap in what Princeton's President Shapiro calls the "shallow ellipse."

Although Scully is the newest dormitory complex on campus, it already plays a complex role that engages most of the university. Its function as a defining edge of the campus has already been mentioned. In addition, Scully and the dormitory that will be built to the west will provide much needed "swing space" as Princeton upgrades and modernizes its large stock of older residential facilities. Upgrading means, of course, everything from wiring for computer terminals to compliance with more stringent fire and accessibility codes. But it also means something more profound than modern infrastructure. It also means re-orchestrating the interior architecture of the existing dormitories to advance a changed perception of what dormitory life should be. Thus, Scully not only serves as "swing space," it is also a prototype for the twenty-first century.

To grasp the nature of the change, it helps to put Scully in the context of what came before. Up until the Civil War, dormitory life at Princeton tended to be Spartan (Nassau Hall, West and East Colleges). This suited a stern Presbyterian temperament not inclined to accommodate the flesh. From the time of President McCosh through the Second World War, dormitory life aspired to a sort of pampered clubbiness—fireplaces, wainscoting, and, in first half of this period, suitable accommodations for one's manservant (Witherspoon, Culyer, 1879 Hall). Princeton had become Anglican. The advent of coeducation in 1969 was both the consequence and the cause of a third major shift. No longer would Princeton's dormitories be a place apart from the world; instead they would be a rehearsal for life in a diverse and complex world. The pendulum had now swung to Congregational. In its most mundane form, this has meant that bathrooms and laundry rooms are no longer afterthoughts stuck in the basement. It has also meant the triumph of the kitchen. As President Shapiro has said: "You study late, you want to be able to warm up a cup of soup."

In short, the design revolution in which Sully Hall is the vanguard is largely internal or programmatic. Here is the future of the university's residence halls—those on the drawing board and those already built, which are being remodeled to conform to the new program. Yes, this means comfortable shared living of the sexes; it means handicap access and a compromise of the traditional system of entries so that residents have an alternative route of escape in the event of fire; it means computer ports and private bath space. It also means rooms for advisors and more public spaces, such as libraries and conference rooms. Compare this to the

Scully Dormitories

domestic rigors endured by Princeton's first students. For the first one hundred years, they had to look after their own needs in everything from food to libraries. The unwritten contract only required the College to provide an education. Students at the beginning of the twenty-first century expect the university to anticipate every need, often under one roof. It is this expectation that is driving and shaping Princeton's growth.

Nothing quite so revolutionary happens on the exterior. That battle was already fought and won by Robert Venturi at Wu Hall. The architects Machado and Silvetti continue Venturi's practice of drawing on Princeton's design history by adopting and adapting a number of its defining character-istics. The great tower and arch have been mentioned, although the appear-ance of Princeton's shield above the arch should be noted. Variety of texture is achieved not by Gothic handcraftsmanship, but by the manipulation of machine-crafted material, including brick of varying sizes (at the arch and the ends of the individual structures of the complex) and, on the south side, precast corrugated panels of gray concrete from which aluminum casement windows jut out like bays. The common room of each the three Scully dorms is painted in a brilliant saturated color that glows in the night like giant semaphores, guiding pedestrians to the red room or the blue room or the green room. The three sides of Scully along with 1922 Hall to the west form the latest in the on-going series of Princeton's great outdoor rooms, here designed by landscape architect Louise Schiller. At this point it looks too bare and open to the elements. But it is the essence of softness itself compared to the way the south elevation confronts (the only possible word) Poe and Pardee Fields. With not so much as a tree, shrub, or bush to medi-ate the psychological gulf between Scully's brutal masonry and the leaves of grass that come right up to its wall, the building projects a factory or warehouse aesthetic. When the sun is at its most brutal, that side of Scully's face must be hotter than the hinges of Hell.

73. Lake Carnegie *Howard Russell Butler '76, 1906*

An architectural tour of the Princeton campus could end with Scully Dormitory. Scully's tower at the green edge of the athletic fields is a defini-tive close to a century that began with the Collegiate Gothic tower of Holder Hall. But to end the story here would be to leave out Princeton's greatest design project, one that is three-and-a-half miles long and up to 800 feet wide.

Lake Carnegie

The tale is delightfully told by the designer, Howard Russell Butler, in an informative book by Gerald Breese, *Princeton University Land: 1752–1984.* Upon graduation, Butler took up a career as a portrait painter. Talent and impeccable social connections opened doors to some of the most glittering inhabitants of the Gilded Age, including Andrew Carnegie (1835–1919), then living in Manhattan. Having been invited by Carnegie to join him on a trip to Princeton to visit former President Grover Cleveland (who had settled there after leaving Washington), Butler shared a dream he had since his days at Princeton. As a student, he been an avid member of the school's crew team, which was far less glamorous than it might sound. At the time, there was no place to row other than the nearby Delaware and Raritan Canal, a dangerous undertaking since the canal was busy with barge traffic. Butler's dream was to "clean out" the marshes (we would call them "wetlands") at the southern edge of the campus and dam the Millstone River at nearby Kingston. The resulting lake would at last provide a satisfactory venue for a winning crew team.

Carnegie was taken by the idea (he was no stranger to creating lakes) and told Butler to work out the cost. Butler first organized the Princeton Lake Committee, chaired by none other than Moses Taylor Pyne. That was his smartest move. He then sought the advice of a professional engineer and provided Carnegie with what he believed to be a fair estimate (which turned out to be hopelessly inadequate) and Carnegie in turn gave his assent to the project—with one stipulation: that Howard Butler should be personally in charge of building it. Woodrow Wilson, who at this time was looking to Carnegie to underwrite his new preceptorial system, had to be content instead with a lake.

Princeton without its lake, the graceful bridges that carry Washington Road and Harrison Street, the surrounding open countryside, and the Class of 1887 Boathouse (Pennington Satterthwaite, 1893) would be a different, more barren place for the loss. The lake and the acres surrounding it (bought largely in secret to prevent price gouging by the owners) provide a buffer that mediates the aesthetic and cultural distance between Route 1 and Princeton University. But the story of the building of Lake Carnegie also provides a snapshot of a remarkable moment in history and helps explain how Princeton was able in a single generation to reinvent itself. It is a story of titanic wills, fortunes, risk-taking, and vision. It is also about something much more difficult to define—a passion, an enthusiasm, a love that redesigned a Victorian pleasure garden into the image of a medieval campus and in the process transformed a regional college into an international university.

Princeton Graduate College

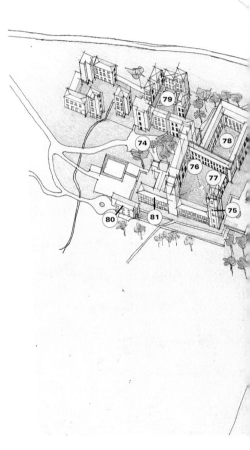

Origins of the Graduate College:
Wilson, West, Cram, and Farrand

> *Bonus entra, melior extra*
> *[Enter good, leave better]*
> —Anonymous, Latin motto, circa 600 AD, inscribed on the mantle
> above the great fireplace in Procter Hall

Princeton's Graduate College was built on the ashes of a failed friendship. In most accounts, President Woodrow Wilson plays the role of doomed liberal hero who wanted to site the Graduate College on the grounds of the under-graduate campus to enrich the intellectual life of the students, while his great antagonist, Dean Andrew Fleming West, assumes the part of imperious conservative hell-bent on building his castle on a site one mile distant from Nassau Hall. It is an engaging script, but the facts are more complex. If there was any wronged party, it was West, not Wilson.

The university's trustees officially established Princeton's Graduate College on December 13, 1900, with West as its first dean. The idea for a graduate program was first broached a century earlier, but it was not until Princeton's sesquicentennial in 1896 that the concept gained a head of steam. That year the trustees decided a Graduate College, the first facility of its kind in the nation, would place Princeton on an equal footing with the world's great universities. Not surprisingly the Philadelphia firm of Cope and Stewardson, which had just completed the widely popular Blair Hall, was commissioned to draw up plans. Published the following year, their concept envisioned an irregular quadrangle entered by an archway similar to that of Blair Tower.

At this point, Wilson and West fully agreed that the graduate college would be a self-contained residential community; there would not be a separate faculty; the style of the architecture would be Collegiate Gothic; and the College would be built in the middle of the undergraduate campus, most likely on a recently acquired parcel north of Prospect House called the Academy Lot. President Wilson then made an unexpected move: he unilaterally appropriated the Academy Lot for his own favored project, the preceptorial program. What was built on the Academy site was not Cope and Stewardson's Graduate College, but McCosh Hall (1907), the classroom building in which Wilson's innovative program was launched. West was stunned; he felt betrayed and realized that by pursuing a site on campus, he and the Graduate School would remain subject to Wilson's priorities. West made up his mind to look elsewhere.

Throughout much of the controversy, consulting architect Ralph Adams Cram backed Wilson. But Cram, along with some alumni and trustees, eventually switched sides in support of an off-campus site, which had the additional advantage of being a blank slate for his High Church theories of architecture. Cram took up the project with a passion born from a conviction that the Graduate College would be one of the works he would be judged by: "I have taken enormous pride in this particular building and have tried to make it not only the best thing we ourselves have ever done, but the most personal as well, and also, if it might be, the best example of Collegiate Gothic ever done in this country." So confident was he about the importance of this project that he made no attempt to downplay the costs. To the contrary, the high pricetag attested to the nobleness of this great enterprise. The Graduate College, he boasted, "shall not cost less than $5,000,000," which at that time was a huge sum.

Was the expense of stained glass, oak wainscoting, and carved lime-stone worth it? *Circumspice.* Nothing quite prepares one for the first encounter with the Graduate College—approaching from the undergraduate campus along College Road, past the golf course, and up the gentle rise to Cleveland Tower, your reach the ceremonial front door, soaring 173 feet above the green and rolling countryside. Less an academic precinct than an English abbey, the emotions evoked during a walk in and through the complex are more likely to be religious than pedagogical—which is what Dean West and his architect intended. If one happens to be there when the 67-bell carillon sounds, the spirituality of the place can be overwhelming.

Cleveland Tower and the rest of the original ensemble of buildings in the Graduate College are the embodiment in brick, limestone, and argilite of deeply held beliefs about the interrelationship between education and architecture. Winston Churchill once observed that we shape architecture and architecture in turn shapes us. Both Dean West and Cram would have said "amen." In the course of designing and building the Graduate College, they worked together as an inspired team in pursuit of a common purpose. "The joy of surroundings that keep [the student] buoyant," West wrote, "means doubling and trebling his power." When they disagreed—which they did—it was over the color of the stone in Wyman House or which craftsman was best for the stained glass of Procter Hall, or the pace of construction on Cleveland Tower. Their disagreements were never about the importance of the work (architecture and education). Both men expected the stones—in their beauty, civilizing influence, and spirituality—to preach sermons to generations of gentleman scholars once they themselves had returned to dust.

Cram and West had been to England. What West saw in the leafy quadrangles of Cambridge convinced him that architecture could affect action and thought; the Medieval towers and great halls of Oxford confirmed for Cram that the style in which the highest moral values resonated was Gothic. In an age of rampant materialism and mechanical standardization, both men saw the Gothic style as an expression of and inspiration for spirituality. It harkened back to medieval Paris and Oxford when both universities were, in West's phrase, "the eyes of Christendom." For both men Gothic architecture was more a principle than a style of design. Like his great medievalist contemporaries in England and France, Cram did not see himself as an antiquarian, but as the standard bearer of a tradition that once brought back to life could equal, if not surpass the achievement of the past.

74. Landscape Masterplan   *Beatrix Farrand, 1912*

Before walking through the Cleveland Tower archway into Thomson College, observe how the curve up the slope slows the pace to emphasize the picturesque. The view of the tower is consistently changing to empha-size its dynamic thrust to the sky. The tower appears, disappears behind trees, then reappears again, a deliberate metaphor for the scholar's halting pursuit of truth. The grove of Douglas fir and white pine on the north side not only serves as a windbreak, but also softens the considerable changes of grade. The trees and shrubs do not crowd the foundation or hide the out-lines of the architecture, but in fact focus the viewer's attention on the build-ings. And at the top of the hill, the land is leveled to form an entrance court defined by a low wall of native stone that continues in front of Cleveland Tower, "making a broad terrace, out of which Cleveland Tower will rise, and giving a quiet base to the line of buildings." The words are those of land-scape gardener Beatrix Farrand.

A study of the architecture on Princeton's undergraduate campus and the Graduate College cannot be lifted out of the context of the land-scape that was designed to receive and complement it. Any appreciation of this most organic art must focus on Farrand. Her work and the rules she established for Princeton's landscape design are as defining an element of

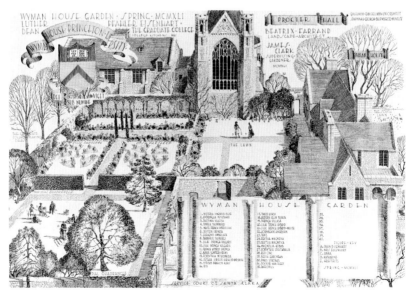

Beatrix Farrand's landscape plan

Blair Arch

the Princeton style as is Collegiate Gothic. Architect Cram, incidentally, was totally against a terrace at the foot of Cleveland Tower; he favored a sloping lawn. Over the years the consensus is that Farrand was right, which illustrates why the picture of Princeton's architecture can be appreciated fully only by looking also at the framing landscape.

Farrand's association with Princeton began in 1912 with the Graduate College. It was a relationship that lasted thirty-two years, most of which she spent as the university's Supervising Landscape Gardener, a position comparable to the one created in architecture for Ralph Adams Cram. A memorial bench and a small garden dedicated to her memory at the northwest corner of Cram's splendid University Chapel offers an insight into the nature of their creative relationship and her unique contribution: Cram and his colleagues sought to lift the spirit; Farrand gave that spirit roots in the nurturing ground.

For an art as ephemeral as landscape architecture, it is a tribute to Farrand's genius and Princeton's enlightened stewardship that so much of her work survives and flourishes. On the undergraduate campus, a few of her masterworks include: the haystack-shaped Japanese yews bordering the flagstone walk leading from the PJ&B train station north to Blair Arch; the great cream-colored blossoms of the specimen *Magnolia grandiflora* on the southwest corner of Pyne Hall; the cascading waves of winter blooming yellow jasmine on the facade of 1901 Hall; the graceful fragrant chains of white and purple wisteria on the east side of Henry and Foulke (woody loops of wisteria vines are a Farrand signature); the flagstone walks that connect the archways of Holder Court and the weeping forsythia espaliered on Holder Hall; the espaliered *Magnolia kobus* on the south wall of McCosh Hall; and the entire precinct around the University Chapel. Even after her relationship with Princeton had ceased, succeeding landscape architects and gardeners have followed the design and planting principles she had laid down. (We can thank Farrand for saying no to that shade tree of last resort, the Norway maple.)

The Graduate College, her first work on any campus, offers the most insight into her philosophy and practice. What she designed around Cram's architecture remains essentially intact, including the two great cedars of Lebanon in Thomson Court, given to Dean West by Farrand's former teacher and director of Harvard's Arnold Arboretum, Charles Sprague Sargent. Her first principle was simple: "A campus is a place for trees and grass, nothing more." Within this basic premise, she developed a practical approach to landscaping that encompassed the big picture. For example, some critics initially considered her plantings around the Graduate College as too sparse. But she understood, unlike many suburban gardeners, that a landscape design factors in time. Plants grow. Her pragmatic approach vetoed designs and materials that would require high maintenance. University budgets simply could not handle such expense. Summer blooming plants were rejected for the sensible reason that no one would be on campus to see them. For this reason, plantings had to maintain their interest in the winter months when classes were in session, which meant attractive shapes, berries, and the occasional evergreen for punctuation. Unless a building was aggressively ugly, plant materials were selected to complement rather than overwhelm the architecture; this included the use of espaliered trees and clipped vines to heighten a particular element such as a bay or the turn of a strategic corner. In every case, plants native to the area were to be preferred.

Above all, Farrand believed that nature was to the spirit what books were to the mind: "We all know education is by no means a mere matter of books, and that aesthetic environment contributes as much to mental growth as facts assimilated from a printed page." Walking through the Graduate College, listen to the dialogue between the architecture (intended to inspire) and the landscape (there to sooth), between stone and leaf, male and female, color and line, the rational and the romantic. The conversation is the key to the power the Graduate College continues to exert.

75. Cleveland Tower *Cram, Goodhue, and Ferguson, 1913*

Although it is easily Princeton's most prominent landmark, it is surprising to learn that this great tower was not part of Cram's original design, but was added at the eleventh hour as a tribute to the twenty-fourth President of the United States, who also happened to be an influential trustee and close friend of Dean West. To pay for all 173 feet of tower, West opened the project to public subscription; no gift was too small, including the pennies of schoolchildren from across the land. The Class of 1892 underwrote as a gift the five-octave carillon, installed later in 1922. (In 1994 the carillon was restored and received the addition of eighty tons of bells.)

Echoing in broad outline Oxford's Magdalen Tower, Cleveland Tower is a striking composition of originality. It seems to revoke the law of gravity; stone rises as if it were lighter than air. The shaft is not a single piece, but divided into four distinct stages, each progressively lighter as the eye rises. Horizontal limestone bands, or stringcourses, define the first two

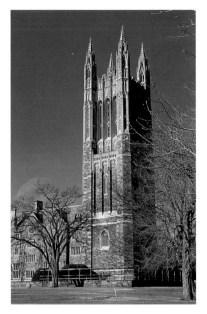

Cleveland Tower

divisions. Each division appears as a sort of booster rocket, launching the next stage into a higher orbit, an effect achieved three ways: by subtly tapering the shaft as it rises; by progressively hollowing out each section, thus reducing the apparent mass, and by altering the proportions of the stone from the rough, darker argilite to the smooth, pale limestone as the tower gains altitude.

The lowest section of the tower is a block of almost solid argilite, save for on each exposed face a single high-pointed window minimally expressed in limestone. The four surfaces of the next section are broken by long and deep limestone incisions. These windows are taller and narrower. The third level, or belfry, is distinguished by an abundance of delicately carved limestone. At the very top, an imaginary rectilinear solid has been largely cut away, leaving only the four pointed corners or the pale limestone pinnacles. Cleveland Tower is an object lesson on the psychology of building tall: such art does not depend on a particular style but the skill of the architect. Perhaps the most impressive feature of this great pile is that for all its size, it does not feed, house, or provide study space for students. It is instead the front door of the college; a memorial to the dean's close friend; and a place to hang tons of bells.

76. Thomson College   *Cram, Goodhue, and Ferguson, 1913*

The most direct entrance into Thomson College, which is the first and oldest of the original closed quadrangles, is through the rib-vaulted passageway to the right of Cleveland Tower. Cram designs an element of surprise by placing the passageway arch not on axis to the court but on the far south side. Seeing only the straight slate path leading to the breakfast rooms in the distance, one has little idea of what is on the other side—the manicured parade ground of the Graduate College. There is also a sense of having entered a self-contained world. The separation or isolation from the world (all the entries open into the quads) is deliberate: Dean West anticipated that graduate students would be from different schools around the world and their fields of study at Princeton would be broad. To confine them to one place, removed from the town and the undergraduates, intentionally created a sort of pressure cooker that would breed solidarity and a sense of

Thomson College

community. "These are the places where the affections linger and where memories cling like the ivies themselves," West wrote in The Graduate College prospectus of 1913, "and these are the answers in architecture and scenic setting to the immemorial longings of academic generations."

Thomson College is a memorial to Senator John Thomson, Class of 1817. The suites housing graduate students (each with its own fireplace) open into outdoor courts, divided into two tiers by a low retaining wall. A characteristic of the Collegiate Gothic style is endless variety: no detail is too small. For the stairs leading to the various entry doors, Cram designed no two quite alike. The separate entries of Thomson College are all connected by a spacious underground passageway that runs around the perimeter. Cram intended the passageway as an unobtrusive route for staff to bring tea or firewood to the residents. Today's *servants* are more mundane: mechanical equipment, recreational space, bathrooms, and various utilitarian services.

77. Thomson Court   *Pyne Tower, and Dean West Statue*

Thomson Court   *Beatrix Farrand, 1913*
Pyne Tower   *Cram, Goodhue, and Ferguson, 1913*
Dean West Statue   *R. Tait McKenzie, 1913*

The north side of the court is penetrated by a cloister over whose exterior wall of Gothic arches loop Beatrix Farrand's omnipresent wisteria. The climbing hydrangea and ivy she planted to emphasize salient angles on the walls throughout the court have likewise been maintained. But the most distinctive impression of Thomson Court's restrained landscape design is the combination of the green squares of the upper and lower lawns with the graceful horizontal blue-green branches of the two great Lebanon cedars. Gazing out to the cedars from the upper level of the quad center stage is the seated bronze statue of Dean West, created by R. Tait McKenzie. Permanently dressed in his academic robes, West looks steadfastly toward the Commons and, slightly to the right, Pyne Tower. The crenellated shape rises above an archway at the east end of Procter Hall, which leads out to the manicured grounds of the Springdale Golf Course. Pyne Tower was designed to house the master of the Graduate College, Howard C. Butler '92, who occupied rooms on the second and third floors. The Commons itself suggests the comfortable worn leather and oak of a distinguished downtown metropolitan club. It serves as the formal parlor where guests are received. Charles Connick, a stained-glass artisan from Boston, designed the armorial medallions that appear on each of the Common Room windows. The seven coats of arms represent the families of men significant to New Jersey's Colonial history, all seven selected by Dean West.

78. North Court *Ralph Adams Cram, 1926*

At the east end of the Thomson Court cloister is a door that opens into a small elegant library. This is among the most pleasant amenities of the North Court, built in 1926 to house the growing number of graduate students. Cram designed North Court with a difference that is experienced as soon as one passes through the archway and gains entry into the quad: the formality of Thomson Court relaxes into a charmingly intimate space. This can be seen from the top of the limestone steps, leading down to a slate

North Court

disk from which paths radiate in a sunbeam pattern to entries around the court. The court is entirely Farrand's design, as are the proportions of the gracious stairs. The one tree, deciduous, in the northeast corner, reinforces the soft quality that contrasts with the stately Lebanon cedars in Thomson Court. The placement of the tree off to the side, not at the center, is typical of Farrand, who favored keeping the center of quads open. The plantings along the margins of the quad are also more varied than those in Thomson Court, including the shape and color of the leaves, and the blossoms and berries. In every instance, their choice and siting is intended to complement rather than upstage the architecture. "Within the quadrangle," Farrand wrote, "only creepers and wall shrubs should be used, as free standing shrubs would tend to destroy the impression of quiet which the buildings themselves give."

79. Procter Quadrangle and Compton Quadrangle
Ballard, Todd, and Snibbe, 1963

Back in Thomson Court, there is a second means of egress at the north, which leads to the modern face of the Graduate College, Procter and Compton Quadrangles. If the spirit of the Cram-West-Farrand complex is High Church, Procter and Compton are pleasantly agnostic.

This is not criticism. Remember what the architects were up against. They were like the proverbial mouse gingerly crawling in bed with a hulking elephant. Continuing to design in a Collegiate Gothic vein was out

Procter Quadrangle and Compton Quadrangle

of fashion—and possibly too expensive. To strike a bold, original note would have been risky; the result could have been the architectural equivalent of a shouting match. It was a moot point, since neither the architects nor the university's administration was possessed by a sense of mission similar to that which had gripped Cram, Farrand, and Dean West. The architects, turning away from Cram's towers and pitched roofs, designed a staggered series of stone and glass cubes stacked two and three stories high.

Although the lack of ornament, the expansive glass windows, flat roofs, and the use of plain geometric shapes in the buildings' plan and elevation identify the residential and social spaces of both quads as undeniably modern, the architects take their cue from the older buildings. Sheathed in the same stone, the residences are arranged as loose quadrangles, with a commons in between. The surfaces are rendered transparent at strategic intervals by large floor-to-ceiling window walls. That much glass is characteristically modern, but the pronounced grey-green vertical framing members suggest traditional mullions. Almost crystaline in the sense of a molecular structure, the two quads appear light and airy at twilight, when the interior electric lights in the rooms are coming on.

Absent is the sense of tight enclosure found in Cram's Thomson College or North Court. Nor is there a manipulation of the grade to convey a sense of walking into or out of a room. More fundamental, there is no attempt to create the illusion that Procter and Compton courts have evolved over time. This is architecture of a very specific moment, not evolutionary. Although the landscaping gives the precinct a parklike air, it is not distinguished by the bold strokes that seem to have come easily to Farrand.

While there are no fireplaces in the rooms or underground passageways to accommodate a servant with tea, Procter and Compton do offer variety in the massing, a deft handling of glass, metal, and stone, and a gently-scaled footprint on the land. The sculpture in Procter Court is Kenneth Snelson's *Northwood II* (stainless steel, 1970); that in Compton Court is *Floating Figure* by Gaston Lachaise (bronze, 1927).

80. Wyman House   *Ralph Adams Cram, 1913; Beatrix Farrand, garden, 1916*

Named after the Graduate College's first benefactor, Isaac Wyman (Class of 1848), Wyman House is the residence of the dean of the Graduate College. Located at the southwest corner of Procter Hall, to which it is linked by a small cloister, Wyman House is a Tudor-style residence meant to complement yet stand modestly apart from the high west gable of Procter Hall. Modest though the stone and half-timbered house might be, Dean West was no less attentive to detail. This is apparent in his correspondence with the contractor: "Wyman House may be less conspicuous and less obtrusive in tone when contrasted with the brighter and richer end of Procter Hall. I

Wyman House

do not mean dark red or brown, but the bluish or purple-black and deep grey tints." When the contractor delivered what West disparaged as "liver-colored" stone, he would have none of it. If contemporary college administrators took this much interest in the details of design and construction, there is little doubt they would be criticized for micro managing. Then as now, architects were not always pleased with what they saw as meddling. Cram was no exception.

While Farrand adhered to restrained design principles for the spaces visited by students, she designed the Wyman House garden as a private and a year-around space. This allowed Farrand to expand her floral palette. Out of this greater freedom came a splendid walled garden on the private north side of the house. The garden, which is appreciably larger than the house, is subdivided into formal outdoor rooms made up of lawns, a shady quadrangle, and parterres planted with seasonal flowers, including roses. Thanks in no small measure to the stewardship of a recent dean of the Graduate College, Theodore Ziolkowski, and his wife, Yetta, the well-loved garden was restored in the 1970s right down to the ivy grown from cuttings from Martin Luther's house in Wittenburg, University College at Oxford, and Christ's College at Cambridge. The ivy of Oxford and Cambridge are at home amid the brick walls of the garden, which incorporate original stonework from both universities.

The jewel in the crown of the Graduate College—its cathedral—is Cram and West's great dining hall. Pairing Dean West with Cram on the design team is no accident; in Procter Hall, West poured out his heart. The son of a Presbyterian minister, West came close to following his father's footsteps. Instead, teaching was his ministry and Procter Hall his church, the armature around which the Graduate College and his educational theories revolved.

A great hall in which the graduate students gathered every night offered the opportunity for a Christian message in a secular space. There would be a High Table—literally on a level higher than the rest of the dining hall—and prayers before every meal. There would also be inspirational talks from the dais to the students in their bachelors robes. Yet the full force of spiritual instruction would not be carried by prayers or lectures, but by the architecture and the related arts—music, painting, wood carving, and most notably stained glass. How successful Cram and West were in designing a non-church church may be gathered by an incident that occurred a few years after the dedication. Industrialist Henry Clay Frick, invited to dinner by Dean West, groused to his host that the space "looked too damn much like a church—all it needs is an organ!" Far from being offended, West leaped at the opportunity to solicit from his guest funds to underwrite the installation of a four-manual organ in the gallery. The organ, completely overhauled in the 1960s, is today one of the University's hidden treasures.

The effect Procter Hall casts speaks for itself. Several features deserve special comment, beginning with the paintings on every wall. West

Procter Dining Hall, wainscoting behind High Table

believed that history was the story of great men rather than impersonal forces or zeitgeists. The juxtaposition, which is deliberate, of the figures in the stained glass and the oil paintings makes the point that the age of heroes continues. The not-so-subtle message is that a life of scholarship and contemplation is equal to the achievement of men of action. At the place of greatest privilege, near the High Table, hang the portraits of such heroes of the Graduate College as Professor Howard C. Butler (the first master of the Graduate College), Francis L. Patton (Princeton's president, 1888–1902, when the concept of the Graduate School was approved by the trustees), and Dean West. Nearby, to the left of Butler is Moses T. Pyne, chairman of the Graduate School Committee. Yet conspicuously absent is a portrait of Woodrow Wilson, an early supporter of the graduate college.

The art of portraiture continues high above in the vaults of the carved wooden ceiling. However, at this altitude, we pass the timber line of heroes into the rarer air of caricature and parody. When you look up, you see a series of wooden beams projecting horizontally from the wall, called hammer beams. More than ornamental, they serve a structural function by spreading the weight of the roof. Look closely: the end of each beam is carved into a human likeness. What these anthropomorphic carvings, each wearing a mortarboard, represent has been a subject of debate since the beginning. With no written proof, tradition has it they represent the trustees

Procter Dining Hall

at the time Procter Hall was built; the key is the objects each holds in his outstretched hands. For example, the figure that holds what appears to be a bar of soap represents trustee William C. Procter (of Procter and Gamble fame).

The magnificent stained glass behind the High Table is by the Philadelphia stained-glass artisan William Willet, a protégé of Dean West; to the left, in the bay at the southwest corner, is the work of Cram's protégé, Charles J. Connick. Under West's guidance, the figures Willet designed convey the message that classical Muses and

Procter Dining Hall

Christian Saints are members of the same mystical family. Two points are made: that there is no inherent conflict between religious and secular education because (and this is the second point) scholarship ultimately leads to a knowledge of God. Lest a scholar succumb to the sin of pride in these glorious surroundings, West would have him ever mindful of the Latin admonition that figures prominently in the glass: *Nec vocemini magistri quia magister vester unis est Christus*, which West translated: "And be ye not called masters, for one is your master, even Christ." Scholars who made a knowledge of God the goal of their learning were, West believed, of all men singularly blessed, a strongly held sentiment that also appears written in the window: "They that instruct many in righteousness shall shine as the stars forever and ever."

Connick's window in the south bay continues and expands on West's gospel that true scholarship is a quest for enlightenment, illustrated by the legend of the Holy Grail as told by Sir Thomas Malory (fl. 1470), which chronicles the search for the cup Christ used at the Last Supper and its final attainment. The lower lancets depict the first appearance of the Holy Grail to Sir Galahad, who is surrounded by the Knights of the Round Table. At a formal dinner in Procter Hall the night before the dedication ceremonies on October 22, 1913, one of the invited foreign dignitaries, Professor Arthur Shipley of Christ's College, Cambridge, remarked as he entered the hall that, "This room was 300 years old the day it was opened." However Professor Shipley meant his words to be taken, as criticism or praise, no higher compliment could have been paid to Dean West and his architect.

Princeton Theological Seminary

The Princeton Theological Seminary or, as it was called until 1958, The Theological Seminary of the Presbyterian Church, was born out of frustration. Princeton's founders had intended the fourth oldest institution of higher learning in the English colonies to be a nursery for ministers of the Gospel—Presbyterian ministers. But almost from the beginning, the College adopted a larger mission, and over the years candidates for the ministry were a declining percentage of those being graduated. Many in the Church's hierarchy were disappointed. In the first decade of the nineteenth century that disappointment grew into alarm.

There was also the issue of student discipline. Under the best of conditions, a large group of young men in tight quarters is a challenge. The particular circumstances of Princeton conspired to keep the students at a slow boil. With few social outlets in a country town and in the face of outright scorn for sports, which would have blown off some steam, the ringing of bells at all hours of the night and the occasional explosion of gunpowder were an undergraduate rite of passage. When more tolerant clerics such as Presidents Witherspoon and Samuel Stanhope Smith were succeeded by strict disciplinarians, pranks festered into periodic riots. The climate was so poisonous that conservative critics of the College blamed students for the fire that destroyed Nassau Hall in 1802.

It was about this time that influential members of the Presbyterian Church and conservative clerics within the College began to agitate for the establishment of a new theological school. The decisive move was made in 1808. It was in the midst of a national evangelical surge called "The Great Awakening" and the need for new ministers of the Gospel was more acute than ever. In that year a minister named Archibald Alexander (1772–1851) petitioned the General Assembly of the Presbyterian Church to establish one or more seminaries. In the brief space of four years Alexander himself was given the task of growing the new institution whose mission was to increase the supply of "enlightened, humble, zealous, laborious pastors to watch for the good of souls."

When the Seminary opened in August 1812 with three students, the occasion was seen by some as a grave threat to the College. The financial support of the Church had been the rock on which Nassau Hall was built. Now much needed funds would be redirected to what was in some respects a rival institution just a few blocks from the Princeton campus. Those fears proved to be well grounded. Until the arrival of James McCosh in 1868, the College was somewhat of an orphan. Not a single new academic facility had been built since Latrobe designed Stanhope and Philosophical Halls (1803).

But in the long run, the separation set in motion the law of unintended consequences. No longer required to toe the theological line of the Church, the curriculum of the College was ultimately free to grow in new directions. (In fact, by the terms of an understanding reached between the College and the Seminary, Princeton was expressly forbidden to hire its own professor of theology.) Time also discovered another advantage: Princeton was largely spared the worst fallout of the occasional doctrinal wars inevitable to men of faith—or at least strong opinions. The first Presbyterian seminary in the western hemisphere would eventually be burdened by both.

Yet separation was not divorce. For many years Princeton remained Presbyterian at its core. At various times, both institutions shared trustees, major donors, and even Presidents. "Of the 20 men appointed as professors at the Seminary up to 1900, they collectively included four who had taught at the College, 10 who were College alumni, 11 who were its trustees, and 10 to whom it awarded honorary degrees, four of whom were awarded two such degrees each," William Selden writes in *The Legacy of John Cleve Green*. Both saw the rise of student eating clubs about the same time and for the same reasons. And both reserved the highest administrative position to ministers cut from Presbyterian cloth. Indeed, it was not until 1902 that the university broke with tradition and selected a president who was not a Presbyterian minister, although Woodrow Wilson's father was a clergyman.

The architecture of the seminary is a testament to this close relationship. William Potter, who figured prominently in the shaping of Princeton's Victorian campus, did important work here, and there are other examples of the architectural conversation between the two.

But the architecture also reflects how the institutions eventually diverged. Most significantly the seminary did not have a Collegiate Gothic phase. There are several reasons why. Collegiate Gothic had been mandated by the university's trustees as part of a larger effort to reinvent the College of New Jersey as Princeton University. There was no similar effort at the seminary to redefine its mandate, which grew increasingly tenacious in defending its image as a bastion of theological conservatism. Also, Collegiate Gothic flourished at a time of dissension and no-growth within the seminary. Yet even if schism and heresy had not been in the air, Collegiate Gothic, which speaks an Anglican vocabulary, would have been inappropriate for the no-frills Reform Christianity the seminary espoused. This is the great watershed after which the architectural histories of the seminary and university flowed in different directions.

During the period of turmoil at the seminary, in the early decades of the twentieth century, some remodeling but no new construction took place. This yielded an unexpected irony: the visitor today looking for the architecture of the university's Victorian past can find it a few blocks to the west at the Princeton Theological Seminary. The seminary enters the twenty-first century with three distinct campuses. None is architecturally related to the other. First, there is the original, historic precinct bounded by College Road, Alexander, and Mercer Streets. Two blocks to the north and west off Stockton Street stands the colonial revival Tennant Campus (designed in the

1920s for the Hun School by architect Rolf William Bauhan and purchased intact by the Seminary in 1943). Finally, some miles to the south between the Delaware and Raritan Canal and Route 1 is the West Windsor campus, a privately-financed 1960s housing complex that went belly up. It was acquired in 1965 for married students through a sheriff's sale. This Walk will be restricted to the original campus, which has the greatest historic and architectural affinity with Princeton University.

82. Alexander Hall *John McComb Jr., 1815; Short and Ford, restoration, 1978*

The seminary walk begins at the beginning, Alexander Hall, originally called Old Seminary. Any question about just how closely the Seminary is related to Princeton University is answered by the architecture of Alexander Hall. The use of local stone; the slightly projecting central bay (both at the front and back) with its oculus at the center of the pediment; the Georgian bilateral symmetry—they all harken back to Nassau Hall as originally designed by Robert Smith and later remodeled by Benjamin Latrobe after the 1802 fire. Indeed, Alexander Hall, the main building and oldest facility of the Seminary, offers a truer picture of the original Nassau Hall (with the exceptions of the 1913 colonial revival cupola and the front doorway) than the Nassau Hall we see today, which was profoundly Victorianized by the architect John Notman.

     True, there are important differences. Alexander Hall has a gable rather than a hip roof. It appears taller (four stories plus English basement as opposed to three) but not so long as Nassau Hall. The one entrance at the front is an original feature as are the two entrances at each side. The

Alexander Hall

two rear doors are much closer to the original configuration of Nassau Hall than one finds today.

Alexander Hall is currently a dormitory. When it opened in 1818, it was, like Nassau Hall, a multi-purpose building with all the seminary's functions under one roof, from a refectory and living spaces for the seminarians to a library and a second-floor chapel or "Oratory." McComb, the architect, is today best known for New York's neoclassical City Hall (1803–12), which he designed with Joseph Francois Mangin. That McComb should have looked back to an eighteenth-century Georgian precedent when he designed the seminary's first building says as much about the continuing power of Nassau Hall as a model for America's colleges as it does about the conservative tastes of his Presbyterian clients.

The selection of McComb, a New York architect, was a break from the pattern that prevailed in the area until the Civil War, when Philadelphia was the venue of choice for design talent. The turn north to Manhattan may be explained by McComb's local connections: he was the son of John McComb Sr., a builder-architect, and Hannah Stockton, a member of one of Princeton's oldest and most prestigious families, the same family that gave the original four acres for the seminary. Thanks to a major restoration in 1978 by the local firm Short and Ford, Alexander Hall is today arguably better than new.

83. Archibald Alexander House and Hodge House

Archibald Alexander House, 58 Mercer Street *1818*
Hodge House, 74 Mercer Street *John Haviland, 1825*

Just as the Princeton campus has two brick houses on either side of Nassau Hall, on either side of Alexander Hall stand Archibald Alexander House and Hodge House. And just as the originally unpainted brick of the university houses (Maclean and Henry) was painted yellow, Alexander and Hodge houses went through a similar metamorphosis.

Like Alexander Hall, Alexander House (which the seminary built for Professor Alexander) is not built in the neoclassical or Federal manner of the period, but is distinctly old fashioned. It looks back to a Georgian past. There is no ornament or delicate detailing. Yet the symmetrical structure has dignity and is surely meant to convey to passersby a useful sense of tradition for an institution that was so new.

By contrast, the contemporary Hodge House seems almost frivolous, perhaps because the architect was a man of international experience who practiced in Philadelphia, then the center of American fashion. Born in England, John Haviland (1792–1854) learned his craft in London. In 1815 he emigrated to Russia, to the young and growing city of St. Petersburg. It was there that he met John Quincy Adams, who was representing the United

Hodge House

States at the court of the Czar. Adams convinced Haviland to re-pack his bags for the even greater opportunities that were sure to await a young architect in America. Arriving in Philadelphia in 1816 with impeccable connections, his reputation took off with the publication of his book *The Builder's Assistant* (1818), one of the earliest illustrated pattern books written and published in North America. In the days when most buildings were designed by talented builder-carpenters, the well-thumbed pattern books were as prized possessions. The popularity of what were in essence recipe books for builders and carpenters explains how a particular style could spread so rapidly over vast distances, even to the reproduction of essentially the same building in different countries. Originality was not the obsession it is today.

Haviland's work for the Seminary's third and perhaps most influential professor, Charles Hodge (1797–1878), was thus an early commission. The most talked about design detail appears above the front door—the faux Palladian window that lets in daylight to illuminate the center hall. The white rays of a stylized sunburst radiating from the window arch is found on no other house in Princeton. Notwithstanding this striking detail, Hodge, like Alexander House, looks back to the earlier Georgian tradition, although the proportions are somewhat lighter and more sophisticated. The kitchen wing to the east, which compromises the closed rectangular shape of the house, is a somewhat later addition. The overall appearance of both houses, especially Alexander, is closer to what Princeton's Maclean House would have looked like as originally designed by Robert Smith.

84. Miller Chapel *John Haviland and Charles Steadman, 1834*

Although Charles Steadman (1790–1868) typically worked from the designs of others, which he readily adapted for his own purposes, he was considered to be the most talented and prolific of Princeton's native architects. Certainly his stamp is everywhere in the buildings that survive from the first half of the nineteenth century. To own or rent a Steadman house today conveys a certain prestige in a town unusually rich in the quality of residential design. The seminary's neoclassical Miller Chapel, with its bold Doric facade, is from his hand. Named for the seminary's second professor, Samuel Miller (1769–1850), the chapel originally faced Mercer Street on a site to the east and somewhat behind Alexander Hall. The seminary, at the time more prosperous than the college, could boast that Miller Chapel opened its doors thirteen years before Princeton could afford its own free-standing chapel (1847), since torn down to make way for East Pyne Hall. If the seminary had followed through and built a planned twin edifice to the west of Alexander Hall, the neoclassical temples would have been the fraternal twins of Whig and Clio Halls on the college campus. They might have even suggested a neoclassical plan for the seminary, similar to that introduced at Princeton by Latrobe and developed by Henry. Yet apart from Miller Chapel, the seminary had no neoclassical phase.

The addition of Miller Chapel to the seminary, along with Alexander Hall and the two adjoining brick houses, gave this campus a compelling presence on Mercer Street. It was a formula the college would adopt under President McCosh. By the closing decades of the nineteenth century, both seminary and college sited new buildings according to a similar pattern: academic facilities were oriented toward the community, and new student facilities faced internally

Miller Chapel no longer has a Mercer Street address. In 1933 the seminary moved, remodeled, and enlarged the building, engaging Philadelphia architects Delano and Aldrich. The new site for this major building suggests that the seminary realigned the campus to focus inward—a contemplative orientation organized around a village green. Miller Chapel was a critical element in the campus's realignment. It became the keystone of two loose quadrangles, defined by Alexander and Hodge Halls to the north and Stuart, Brown, and the Administration Building on the south.

The chapel's restoration involved removing such Victorian additions as stained-glass windows, installed in 1874, and returning to what was perceived to be a more theologically and aesthetically appropriate clear glass, a re-created hand-rolled (rather than commercially produced) glass,

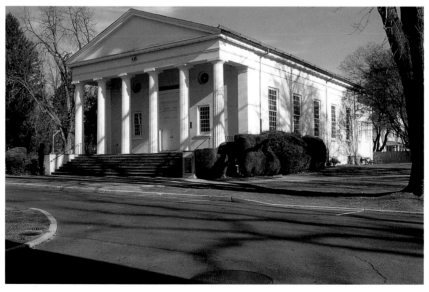

Miller Chapel

which has the delicate lavender tint of old glazing. Much of the interior, including the chancel, dates from this restoration, although the gallery parapet and the supporting columns are the original work of Steadman.

Current plans call for yet another restoration. This raises all the obvious questions about what precisely is being restored when a building's history is a succession of important architects. This does not even touch on accommodating heating, cooling, lighting, and security technologies unimagined when the building was first designed, as well as life safety and handicap access now mandated by federal law.

85. Stuart Hall   *William A. Potter, 1876; remodeling and restoration, 1980s*

When William A. Potter, the architect of Princeton's Chancellor Green Library, turned his hand to Stuart Hall, he designed this splendid Venetian Gothic classroom facility to front on Alexander Street. Anyone walking or riding from the train station to the seminary would see Stuart's gabled tower topped by finials poking like an arrow through the canopy of trees. It was an impressive signpost, leading to the front door of Stuart and the seminary campus. Claiming structural concerns, the seminary removed the tower in the 1950s. A more plausible explanation for the amputation was that the administration saw little reason to invest in restoring a piece of ornament; certainly not when there were pressing needs to build a student center and to modernize a physical plant that had received little attention during the Depression and World War II. Nor did it help that after decades of neglect, Victorian architecture was viewed nationally as hopelessly ugly.

When it was built, Stuart Hall was celebrated for the workmanship and the use of building materials. Contemporary critics found it "massive, beautiful and imposing." A century later, a 1980s restoration corrected years of neglect and scrubbed off generations of grime, rediscovering for a new generation the former luster of Stuart Hall. Here are all the familiar traits that are the delight of Victorian architecture: the ornament, the color, and the uniformity within the exuberant variety. The windows of each story follow one architectural style and shape, yet the aesthetic deck is reshuffled from floor to floor. The carved floral motifs at the west entrance are lush to the point of appearing tropical. There is the love of natural light expressed in the ample glazing that punctuates the brownstone masonry, which renders the stone almost lacy. And there is the piling on of different materials, from the encaustic tile floor of the street-side entry porch to the limestone-edged windows and the polished marble pillars that support the entry arches.

All this exuberance might deceive the contemporary viewer into believing that ornamentation was the primary motive guiding the Victorian

Stuart Hall

architect's hand. This was seldom the case and certainly not true of Potter, who adeptly designed mechanical systems—ventilation, natural lighting, and fireproofing—in consideration of both functional and aesthetic interests. Inside, the entry hall is bracketed by a pair of wooden staircases that lead to the upper floors, positioned in the middle of the building to pull fresh air through the building, up and out of the towers. High ceilings in the lecture rooms and large operable windows amplify the effect.

An interesting footnote to the history of Stuart Hall is that the donors, the pious Stuart brothers (who gave Prospect House to the college for President McCosh's use), made their gift conditional on the seminary honoring in perpetuity several points of Presbyterian doctrine. If any Stuart heir were to catch the seminary in some theological lapse, every tile, finial, and polychrome arch would revert to the family.

86. Brown Hall *J. B. Huber, 1865*

South of Stuart Hall fronting College Road is Brown Hall, designed by architect J. B. Huber of Newark, New Jersey. It was the first single-use dormitory on the seminary campus, constructed to house an influx of students on the eve of the Civil War. Like Alexander Hall, Brown was built of local stone; the four-story elevation is basically Georgian; and the exterior corners are emphasized by quoins (evenly cut blocks of different stone of different color). The deep white portico, which shelters the front entrance, is a neoclassical rather than Georgian detail. This and the somewhat over-scaled cupola, which looks like a classical pavilion, identify Brown Hall as a

Brown Hall

building of the mid-nineteenth century, although still somewhat conventional for a late Civil War building.

Brown Hall is named for the donor, Mrs. George Brown of Baltimore. A few years after it opened, the building was equipped with gas heat for which the students each paid $10 a session. In 1880 bathrooms were installed. Recent upgrades have included central air conditioning and cable wiring as well as Internet access. The New Jersey Historical Commission awarded the careful exterior renovation, completed in 1994, first prize.

87. Administration Building

John Notman, 1847; renovated and enlarged, 1981

Opposite Brown Hall to the north is the Administration Building. One rule of collegiate architecture is that even when a building outlives its original purpose, it is seldom torn down. Instead, the school reprograms it to meet current needs. Yet no other building on this or the Princeton campus has had so many identities. Notman designed the modest single-story stone building to house the seminary's refectory and infirmary. Like the college, the seminary's kitchen was not up to the task and eventually closed in 1899. The building was then used as a dormitory. A decade later the students were moved out and athletic equipment moved in to what then became the new gymnasium. By 1945, after the seminary had purchased the nearby Hun School property, which had a more modern gym, the building became the

Administration Building

seminary's executive arm, housing offices of the president and the academic dean.

A simple structure can accommodate these radical transformations more easily and far less expensively than, say, a Stuart or Brown Hall. The Administration Building, both, the original structure and the large wing on the south side, is that kind of background building. Best known for his Italianate work on the Princeton campus, Notman designed here in a restrained and somewhat old-fashioned neocolonial mode.

88. Mackay Campus Center *George Licht, 1952*

The building that closes off the west side of the informal quad formed by the Administration Building, Stuart, and Brown Halls is Mackay Campus Center. Ever since the original refectory had closed at the end of the nineteenth century, the seminary was desperate for a centrally located facility in which students could eat and socialize. It is a familiar theme. Like the seminary, the university wrestled with the same issue for over two centuries. And like Princeton, hungry seminary students reacted the same way—they set up eating clubs. Again like Princeton, the seminary's administration was concerned the eating clubs worked against a sense of community. Not having a place in which to sit down to eat together, not to mention the lack of meeting space that could be used by the students and outside groups, were nagging problems the seminary had to address. Mackay met both needs quite nicely; Princeton is still finding its way. The eating clubs, no longer needed, closed, and the bookstore finally had a home; and the seminary had a facility for outreach. Moreover, the construction project proved to be a welcome sign of new energy: after a hiatus of nearly sixty years, the seminary was building again.

But here is the rub: why does Mackay Campus Center have to look like a standard-issue welcome center on the Interstate highway? By alluding to the neo-Georgian tradition of Alexander Hall, Mackay calls unwanted attention to just how uninspired it is, right down to the difference between the wonderfully warm local stone of the older building and the Campus Center's bland manufactured brick. Was it funds? A lapse of taste or talent? Or the timid, conventional *zeitgeist* of the 1950s that knew the world had changed, but wasn't quite sure how to creatively respond? An argument could be made that advances in the technology of building systems, especially heat, ventilation, and lighting, made architects and clients lazy.

Stairwells with operable windows, for example, were no longer necessary so long as there was a socket into which one could screw a bulb or, worse, a fluorescent tube. A new building could be an impenetrable, hermetically sealed block. For that matter, it could be built underground. Nor did the contemporary architect have to site a building just so to capitalize on ambient light and prevailing breezes. All those Victorian towers, which did double-duty as airshafts, were no longer needed. What was left in many cases was the decorated box, which is the essence of the Mackay Campus Center—a brick box tricked up in colonial revival wrappings.

On the other hand, why should anyone care what a building looks like so long as it performs exactly how the architect intended and the client hoped? But that raises an issue that runs throughout this book: is the value of architecture largely judged by how well it accommodates human activity? Or does architecture make a larger, more assertive claim on one's thoughts and emotions? Individuals as different as Princeton's Dean West and Walter Gropius, the founder of the Bauhaus, believed they knew the answer.

The seminary's Campus Center skirts the issue by literally hanging inspirational material on the walls. The brick porch at the front of the Campus Center, with its rounded arches, might well be called the porch of the martyrs. On bronze plaques are names of the seminary's illustrious dead whose ultimate sacrifice continues to bear witness to their faith: Elijah Parish Lovejoy, Class of 1834, died protecting his printing press from mob attack; James Joseph Reeb, Class of '53, was fatally beaten in Selma, Alabama; the Reverend John Alexander Mackay, the seminary's third president, 1936–1959, was the Center's most ardent advocate and namesake.

89. Hodge Hall   *Robert H. Robertson, 1893*

Hodge Hall occupies the site of a wooden gymnasium, Langdonic Hall, which the students built for themselves in 1859, a period when the seminary like the college put little stock in the "sound body, sound mind" view. As the last of the major nineteenth-century buildings on the original campus, Hodge Hall has a footprint that looks like an enormous stone L, with a round tower joining the two uneven wings like a great masonry hinge. The shape is yet another creative example of how late-nineteenth-century architects addressed related concerns of daylight and ventilation at a time when neither was easily accommodated by flipping a switch to turn on a light or start a fan. In this instance, the architect was aided by an enlightened donor who stipulated that every room should have sunlight at some point in the day. As for ventilation, the high ceilings of the rooms, the French doors at the ends of the halls, the operable transoms over the first-floor windows, and the central staircase within the tower—all contributed to a constant supply of fresh air.

Hodge Hall

Unlike Stuart Hall, built twenty years before, Hodge Hall looks to the simpler lines of early American architecture, rather than Romanesque or Gothic revival. "Simpler" is a relative term. First there is the central tower with its crown of windows. Also, the rounded arches of the windows of the top story, the windows at the grooved or chamfered corners of the wings (not to mention the chamfered corners themselves), and the paired grouping of windows—all manifest a late-nineteenth-century affection for extracting order out of picturesque complexity. Time has robbed the struc- ture of some of its variety. Early photographs reveal large chimneys, which have been removed, no doubt to prevent fire once central heating had been installed; also, at the roof line of the side entrances there appear to have been decorative arches that lead nowhere. It is not difficult to imagine what happened to these under the assault of weather.

It is the rusticated granite and brownstone that reveal the Victorian heart and soul of Hodge Hall. From the irregularly sized pink- granite blocks that play against the regular brownstone quoins; to the hori- zontal bands of darker stone that deflect rainwater from the wall (and offer a visual clue to the division between the floors); the brownstone spandrel panels between the windows of the top two floors; and the brownstone cornice under the eaves of the green slate roof—this is a building that cel- ebrates the craftsmanship of the mason.

Originally a dormitory for men, Hodge Hall was renovated in the 1960s to also house women and married couples. The building was remod- eled in 1980, providing facilities for about 70 students in single rooms and three-room suites. Yet another remodeling in 1989, this time of the first floor, resulted in offices for faculty members. Recent work on the exterior is a textbook case of late-twentieth-century technology—scientific restoration. The mortar between the stone, for example, was not simply replaced; it was chemically analyzed to reveal its original color when built; when replaced, the mortar was applied in such a way as to reproduce the original rounded or "bullnose" effect.

The building honors the memory of one of the most eloquent nineteenth-century Calvinist theologians, Charles Hodge (1797–1878). His brand of conservative theology is perhaps best summarized in his own words: "I am not afraid to say that a new idea never originated in the Seminary.... The Bible is the word of God. That is to be assumed or proved. If granted; then it follows, that what the Bible says, God says. That ends the matter."

90. Templeton Hall   *Ewing, Cole, Cherry, and Parsky, 1989*

Templeton Hall

Like Mackay Campus Center, the newest academic facility on the seminary's original campus also harkens back to an ersatz eighteenth-century Colonial past. Besides providing classrooms and administrative offices, it houses a state-of-the-art communications and media center. Yet nothing about the exterior offers a clue of the sophisticated business going on inside.

Templeton shows greater agility than Mackay, if not imagination, in reviving neocolonial forms. The warm colors of the square masonry are easy on the eye, and the gabled entry pavilion is a more compelling front door than the rounded arches of Mackay's shadowy porch. Even the cupola looks as if it were designed especially for this roof, compared to the off-the-shelf stock item perched atop Mackay. But Templeton is vexed by its own devils. There is something tense about the elevation. As one approaches from the east, Templeton appears to be a relatively modest three-story structure, but the site drops away sharply and the entrance is a sort of bridge at the second floor. Up close, you see that the first floor sits in a moat. The slope might have been an opportunity for a creative design solution, rather than a problem the architects could not overcome.

Springdale Hall

A short walk from Templeton leads to Frog's Hollow and Springdale Hall at 86 Mercer Street. Since 1903 the official residence of the President of the seminary, Springdale was built in 1846 for Richard Stockton, the eldest son of Commodore Robert Stockton. Although there is no definitive evidence, the architect is thought to have been John Notman, the man who designed the university's Prospect House. Springdale is a transitional building. It eddies charmingly at the intersection of several contemporary currents. The elevations of the individual pieces come close to the proportions of a classical revival temple. Yet the deep eaves with their prominent brackets read more like the Italianate architecture for which Notman was famous. On the other hand, the crenellated parapets on the bays, the diamond-shaped mullions, and the decorative molding over the windows are characteristically Gothic details. It is a picturesque composition. Clearly the client commissioned a residence that would ingratiate rather than overwhelm. It is just the sort of house an English vicar and his daughters might inhabit in Jane Austin's world.

92. Speer Library and Henry Luce III Library Addition

Speer Library *G. A. and G. T. Licht and O'Connor and Kilham, 1958*
Henry Luce III Library Addition *Alan Chimacoff, 1992*

The most important architectural story in the neighborhood around Springdale is about the buildings that are not there. In 1843 nearly forty years before Princeton could afford a library, the seminary built Lenox Library, named for James Lenox, a wealthy book lover from Manhattan; this wonderful Gothic Revival structure survives only in a few stones and some old photographs. Similarly, if you look for a second and later library (1879), which stood immediately behind the original building—a red brick, high Victorian edifice designed by Richard Morris Hunt, one of America's most popular nineteenth-century architects—here, too, you will have to consult old photographs. Both were torn down in the 1950s to make way for Speer Library.

When word of the Seminary's intentions to demolish both libraries leaked out, the list of community residents who opposed the demolition included the eminent scientist Albert Einstein. Nevertheless, this was the 1950s. Historic preservation was in its infancy and there were few laws to protect our architectural heritage. Both buildings were razed. The buildings'

Speer Library

loss was a wake-up call that raised the consciousness of town and gown alike to their architectural treasures and laid the foundations for a broad-based preservation ethic. In memorium, four stones from the old Lenox Library are embedded in the wall to the right of the Mercer Street entrance.

The Alabama limestone buildings that replaced these historic facilities are functionally a great improvement. Speer in particular benefited from the pioneering work of the architects of Princeton's Firestone Library, O'Connor and Kilham, who acted as consultants on the interior. But the plan and elevation of Speer are disappointing. The building straddles uneasily the ground between a stripped-down neoclassicism (there is geometric symmetry) and Gothic revival (the entry tower and the bare suggestion of buttresses). But it arrives somewhat surprisingly at what seems to be a 1940s take on art deco. There are gestures throughout that try to delight the eye, but the building stays relentlessly earth bound. Like the double row of decorative low-relief sculptures on the tower that represent essential Christian truths, they may well be truths, but rigidly formatted and stacked one on top of another, they hardly inspire.

As for the Luce addition, which was chosen in a design competition, it too serves the seminary well as a repository for rare books and manuscripts (the William H. Scheide Center) and as a center for computerized resources. From the outside it lacks even the grudging amenities of Speer. Chimacoff's fixed trapezoidal windows sans mullions over the entrance are assertively postmodern. What the blocked up windows on the north side facing Lenox House are saying is more difficult to figure out.

It is hard to imagine there would be much outcry from the community if fifty years hence the current libraries were to face demolition. Even so, the scholars who use both Speer and the Luce addition would likely rise up in its defense. A temple to knowledge or a knowledge factory? It is an issue the architects of libraries are struggling with the world over. The older libraries were often structures of great beauty cherished by their communities. The newer facilities are better attuned to the information revolution, yet seldom inspire much affection. If the architects of the seminary and Princeton libraries do not match the visual aesthetics of their predecessors, they are by no means alone.

Lenox House

This house, at the corner of Library Place and Stockton Street, is another example of James Lenox's generosity to the seminary. At one point it belonged to a group of three houses that faced Stockton Street. These, however, fell victim to a uniquely twentieth-century urban cancer—parking lots. The aesthetic parents of Lenox House are the Arts and Crafts movement and the late-nineteenth-century American stick style, whose forms tend toward the simpler articulation of masses that would become popular toward the end of the century. The hipped eaves and dormers, porches, and painted brick are characteristic details. Whereas the seminary has carefully preserved the exterior of the house, the inside has been pretty much cut up to house the offices of various research efforts, such as the Dead Sea Scrolls Project.

94. Carriage House *circa 1826; moved, 1909; remodeling, 1967*

So much has been said about what has been lost to inattention, neglect, and poor judgment, that it seems fitting to end this tour of the old campus and nearby precincts with the Carriage House. The building began its life nearby as a stable for Thompson Hall, a great house that had been located at 50 Stockton Street. In 1909 the Carriage House was transported to its present location on Mercer Street between Speer Library and the Trinity Church parking lot. The seminary bought the building in 1967 and extensively remodeled the interior to house faculty offices.

Because architecture belongs not just to the moment of inception, but to its dialogue with time, one of the most creative, nurturing voices can be that of enlightened stewardship. In this regard, the architectural history of the seminary is today adding new chapters that although subtle and not always immediately visible to the casual passerby are in their way a record of outstanding achievement. The painstaking technologies of modern historic preservation are being applied by the seminary to protect a precious and irreplaceable heritage. This attitude of stewardship, which is also shown in the care of the park-like landscaping that enriches the historic precinct, is evidence of an admirable commitment to pass intact to future generations a legacy that will not only continue to teach, but will also continue to delight.

Institute for Advanced Study

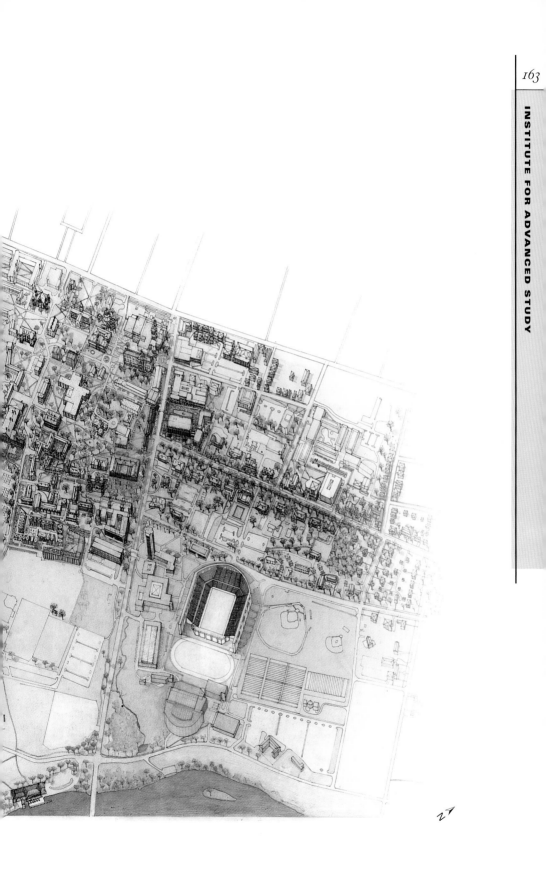

Before and long after its founding on May 20, 1930, timing has played an important role in the meteoritic ascent of the Institute for Advanced Study, the first institution of its kind in the United States. The enlightened philanthropy of the Institute's benefactors, Louis Bamberger and his sister, Mrs. Felix Fuld, was made possible by the fortuitous sale of their retail business to R. H. Macy & Company just weeks before the 1929 stock market crash—before businesses and asset prices cratered. Mrs. Fuld and Mr. Bamberger had intended to support a new medical school in Newark. Toward that end, they sought guidance from Abraham Flexner, an international authority on medical education. Dr. Flexner, however, 64 years old and looking for new challenges, responded by convincing them to support a very different kind of project—a model center for post-doctoral research and the art of teaching, rather than a medical school. He also persuaded them to shift their sights slightly to the south and west to Princeton.

The 350-acre farm tract on which the Institute was eventually built was intended to offer scholars and teachers a retreat from the distractions of the world. But the world was not so easily ignored in the late 1920s and 1930s. The rise of Fascism and Nazism sent many of Europe's most distinguished scientists and educators packing to America. For them, the Institute for Advanced Study, rather than an experiment, became a safe haven for what soon became an outstanding faculty, headed most conspicuously by Albert Einstein (1879–1955).

Flexner and his associates understood that the Institute's architecture, more than simply housing faculty and administration, should express the Institute's intellectual ideals, financial viability, and confidence in the future. These same principles guided Dean West twenty years before when he built Princeton's Graduate College, the first institution of its kind in this country. But whereas Dean West looked back to what he viewed as a nobler tradition, Flexner looked to the present and future:

> …a university like all other human institutions—like the church, like governments, like philanthropic organizations—is not outside but inside the general social fabric of a given era.…It is…an expression of the age, as well as an influence operating on both present and future.

Modern design, or the international style of architecture, was most expressive of the age in which the Institute was founded. To modernists, pure geometric forms and straight lines were more than simply rational; they were more honest; they celebrated the machine aesthetic. Flexner's commitment to stripped down, utilitarian modernism was reinforced by a paradox of American higher education: Princeton and other universities often housed underpaid faculties in splendid facilities. He spoke out against institutions that emphasized bricks over salaries: "Glorious buildings, gothic, neo-gothic, colonial, concrete stadia...student buildings of elaborate design, constructed while the college or university is pleading its inability to pay decent salaries." Such institutions had their priorities backwards.

As Flexner saw it, an enlightened educational institution pursued an architectural program that focused on function, amenity, and cost. The faculty's needs would always be uppermost. His views would ultimately guide his successors to build in a way different from the university or the seminary. The Institute was neither burdened by the past nor dependent on precedent; it was free to build in a new direction. Now, after seventy years, the Institute for Advanced Study can hardly be called a new idea. Yet its history, as revealed through the work of the leading architects of the second half of the twentieth century, shows a continuing commitment to reexamine new building projects within the constraints of function, amenity, and cost. Unlike campuses that have sprung from the mind of a single designer, the Institute has evolved over time, adding a new building about every decade. The collection is stylistically heterogeneous, ranging from colonial revival to post- and neomodernism, and the parts hang together. They add up to an educational community that continues to be, as the first director, Abraham Flexner, intended, "an expression of the age, as well as an influence operating on both present and future." It is a place where man and nature are collaborators rather than adversaries. If you stand quietly, looking north toward Fuld Hall across the lake that occupies the middle distance, you can hear a dialogue between the campus and the woods. It is a conversation between fast and slow time, change and permanence, and the theories of man and the practice of nature on this gentle site.

95. Fuld Hall   *Jens Fredrick Larson, 1939*

When the *New York Times* first carried the story of the proposed new Institute for Advanced Study, leading architects wasted no time contacting Flexner. This was, after all, the Depression. Letters poured in from traditionalists and modernists alike. By turning to Larson (1891–1982) for its first building, the Institute chose one of the leading contemporary designers of collegiate architecture. He was largely self-taught architect (when such a thing was still possible), and began his career in college design at Dartmouth in 1919 as architect in residence. Larson also had a major impact on the architecture and the campus plans of Colby College, Bucknell, Lafayette, and Wake Forest.

The Georgian revivalist style of Fuld Hall might come as something of a surprise in light of the Institute's modernist vision. Flexner, however, had a more immediate concern: the Institute needed instant credibility.

Fuld Hall

Potential donors, as well as faculty and students, were more likely to sign on to a school designed in a familiar, traditional idiom. Larson gave the Institute the illusion of historical roots. He also implied a prestige in its relationship to Princeton University by recalling the Georgian outlines of Nassau Hall. An additional impulse peculiar to the years just before World War II was a renewed interest in America's colonial past, reflected in the re-creation of Colonial Williamsburg in Virginia.

Larson's approach to design would be called *contextual* if he were practicing today. "One should not copy an old existing building and adapt life to that building," he wrote, "but, with a vocabulary that study gives, should envisage the contemporary problem and clothe it in traditional architecture." In other words, the way a building works internally should be a state-of-the-art response to the life inside, whether that activity is a lecture on Kant or a scientific experiment for cloning sheep. But the box in which this activity takes place should be covered, according to Larson, in a design that communicates the *idea* of a college—in the same way a steeple communicates the idea of a church. This points up the challenge the modernists faced on campus: they had to create a new language that also communicated a traditional idea.

Fuld Hall's colonnaded porch, leading to a pair of symmetrical two-story brick pavilions, recalls Latrobe's siting in 1802 of Philosophical and Stanhope Halls at Princeton's Nassau Hall. Larson also imposed a Beaux-Arts scheme on the rolling farmland by lining up the director's house (the eighteenth-century country home of the Olden family) as the northern terminus of a north–south axis running through Fuld's cupola. Incidentally, the cupola's three-part massing—square base, rectangular shaft, and circular capped lantern—echoes the cupola atop Independence Hall in Philadelphia, including the wooden urns and clock. Perhaps the

Olden Manor

reference was simply decorative; perhaps, on the eve of the impending Second World War, Larson intended a patriotic gesture.

Like the first buildings at the university (Nassau Hall) and the seminary (Alexander Hall), Fuld Hall was an all-purpose facility. It originally housed the Institute's administrative functions, seminar rooms, lounges, a library, and dining rooms. Today, it contains administrative and faculty offices as well as the mathematics library. Unlike Nassau and Alexander, Fuld did not have living quarters; the older resident students, many married, were responsible for their own housing. Nor, presumably, did the resident fellows require the services of a chapel.

96. Buildings C, D, and E *Matthew C. Fleming, 1948–1953*

The outbreak of World War II put all construction on hold. After the war, scarce materials, craftsmen, and funds permitted only basic maintenance and a modest building program. In 1948 the Institute put up a pair of two-story neocolonial structures, a short distance from the rear of Fuld. Called buildings "C" (at the southeast corner) and "D" (at the southwest), these two mirror image rectangular blocks extended Larson's Beaux-Arts plan and suggested the beginnings of a large open quadrangle. In 1953 Princeton architect Matthew C. Fleming added a third neocolonial brick building, "E," located south and east of building "C." Rotated 90 degrees from the north/south orientation of Buildings "C" and "D" and placed considerably to the east of the prevailing grid, it remains unclear whether the siting was a matter of convenience or if a Building "F" was intended to face building "E."

Whatever the plan, a major change in stylistic direction was in the works. To the east of the main campus, across Olden Lane, Flexner's modernist program for the Institute was at last about to be realized. The turning point came as the Institute addressed its most glaring deficiency—affordable housing for resident scholars. Without this, the Institute could not truly foster a sense of community.

97. Fellows Housing   *Marcel Breuer, 1957*

As early as 1945, the Institute asked Alfred Barr, the influential director of New York's Modern Museum of Art, for recommendations of modernist architects. Among those he named (for what Barr characterized as a "rather uninteresting problem") were the young Philip Johnson (1906–) and Louis Kahn (1901–1974). Twelve years passed before the project advanced from discussion to actual construction. But when ground was at last broken in 1957, the man chosen to design the Fellows Housing was one of the most widely acclaimed modernists, Marcel Breuer (1902–1981).

A native of Hungary, Breuer was part of the wave of intellectuals and artists who fled fascism in the 1930s. After several years at Harvard University with his fellow emigre and founder of the German Bauhaus, Walter Gropius (1883–1969), Breuer moved to New York City in 1947 to open his own practice. An acclaimed educator, author, furniture designer, and recipient of the AIA's Gold Medal in 1968, Breuer today is perhaps best known for his graceful caneback tubular chair. His name is also associated with a style of architecture pejoratively if not aptly called Brutalism. In his own day Breuer was especially admired for the clean lines of his residential design and thus was an obvious choice for the Institute's break with revivalist architecture.

As originally designed, the twenty buildings of Breuer's housing complex constitute a fascinating amalgam of quintessentially 1950s American and European impulses. Here is the European affection for balconies and communal living wedded to the American love of patios and breezeways. Indeed, the most prominent feature of the front elevation is certainly not the high strip windows (for privacy), but that icon of suburbia,

Fellows Housing

the large carports. These serve triple duty: they shelter the car; break up the facade to provide vistas through the building; and, the two-story roof decks function as porches for the occupants upstairs.

The one- and two-story grouped housing recites a familiar stripped-to-the-bones modernist vocabulary, with orange brick end walls and painted tongue-and-groove cedar siding. Open exterior stairways, roof overhangs, and sunshades vary the surface texture on front and back. Breuer creatively manipulates light, shadow, and air circulation for the benefit of the residents inside. The buildings sit atop concrete pads, the need for basements eliminated by a central heating plant and a community laundry room. Although the automobile plays a dominant role in the design and life of Fellows Housing, the complex is oriented inward rather than out to the public street. The buildings are clustered to define loose courts or quadrangles. These clusters are sited around a central grassy open space, which serves as a village green of sorts. If you are looking for life, walk around to the rear and into the tree-shaded quads.

Since Breuer directs human activity to the private space out back, and since that activity is likely to be the children of resident families, the kitchen, dining, and living rooms face out to the courts. Windows (including the single-pane glass door opening to a small flagstone patio) are appropriately generous—the better to keep an eye on the children while coffee brews. Bedrooms and study areas tend to be grouped toward the street on the front. The parklike setting of mature trees and grass is pleasant enough, but there is little evidence to suggest that the services of an inspired landscape architect have been engaged.

Breuer offered the resident fellows and their families five floor plans. All the rooms of a given unit were situated on one level and each unit had a fireplace. The word "kitchenette" offers a good sense of how the space was used in the years before the kitchen became the social gathering place of most American houses. Also, Breuer minimized closet space, in response to a perception that scholars and their families were acetic sorts.

An enthusiastic contemporary profile of the project in *Architectural Record* (March 1958) reported that a variety of building shapes were considered during design. But when, as here, the basic form is replicated twenty times, and the veneer is low cost (stock brick and wood paneling), the result is really a more thoughtful version of a suburban garden apartment. Yet for all the apparent simplicity of these machines for living, Breuer was in fact nudging the envelope of construction technology. Shortly after residents moved in, a problem arose: the flat roofs, internal drainage, and radiant heating in the ceiling caused such leaks that gabled roof structures had to be slapped on to the buildings. The resulting incongruity compromised the clarity of the original design. Fortunately, that was not the last word. The Institute has engaged architect Michael Landau to renovate and upgrade the entire housing complex. Internal modifications include everything from new

wiring to accommodate contemporary information technologies, to a complete reworking of the tight kitchenettes. These are being expanded into breakfast rooms that break through the plane of Breuer's original rear elevation and step modestly into the courts as square bays. The architect is also re-creating Breuer's flat roofs, restoring much of the pleasing shock the housing must have had for its first residents.

98. Social Sciences and Historical Studies Library

Wallace K. Harrison, 1965

Nearly a decade was to pass before the Institute built again. But the Breuer project had set a precedent that was brilliantly confirmed with the construction of a new library for the Schools of Social Sciences and Historical Studies. Initially the Institute's trustees turned again to Breuer. But they rejected the proposal he offered and the Institute's director, Robert Oppenheimer (1904–1967), contacted Wallace K. Harrison (1895–1981), an old family friend.

The modernist firm of Harrison and Abramovitz is best known for its work on the plan of the United Nations and Lincoln Center, both in New York City. For these, Harrison was the indispensable glue that somehow held together inherently unstable consortiums of star architects. Harrison's reputation was that of a manager who could get things done. But as the Institute's library makes clear, his talents were not limited to orchestrating the work of others; Harrison was quite capable of performing a star turn on his own and in fact received the AIA Gold Medal in 1967.

Social Sciences and Historical Studies Library

The library is born out of the modernist international style. The geometry is rectilinear; the walls are great expanses of glass; the coffered eaves are deep and overhanging; and the roof appears flat. (More on that in a moment.) Fully appreciative of the natural beauty on all sides, especially the small lake to the south, Harrison gently eases the building into the shoulder of the westward sloping site. Standing to the east of the library, it appears to be a relatively modest single-story structure that hugs the ground. Stepping around to the south or west elevations reveals that the library is two stories. Yet even here, the building does not overwhelm the setting. The fieldstone base, the wood panels on the upper story, and the broad white cornices convey the domesticity of an American prairie style house. The intended transparency of the expansive glass surfaces was somewhat compromised, however, when an amber-colored film was laminated to the inside surface of the glass to cut down heat loss (or gain) and glare.

The most striking design gesture is initially invisible. It is up on the roof. Standing on the outside during daylight hours, one is aware of a soft ambient light that bathes the inside of the library but cannot identify the source. Once inside, it turns out the roof is a parallel series of east/west coves, the north sides of which are faced by clear glass. The effect is like standing at the bottom of a pool of water looking up through breaking waves. The challenge of protecting paper-based collections from direct sunlight without cutting off the outside world is here solved in a way that can only be called beautiful. Of course the roof leaks. Except for the challenges this poses for the librarian, this is one building where the architect can be forgiven for achieving delight rather than perfection.

99. Dining Hall and West Building

Robert L. Geddes of Geddes Brecher Qualls Cunningham;
Zion & Breen, landscape architects, 1969

The Institute for Advanced Study is organized as a collection of schools. There are currently four: historical studies, mathematics, natural sciences, and social studies. All were initially housed under a single roof in Fuld Hall. Thus, the history of new construction at the Institute has been about designing appropriate facilities to accommodate each school as it developed and grew. In 1968 the Philadelphia firm of Geddes Brecher Qualls Cunningham (GBQC) prepared a masterplan for the Institute, which identified proposed sites for the next generation of facilities and outlined four guidelines for future growth: respect for the existing landscape, development of courtyards and quadrangles, implementation of rational circulation patterns, and creation of new facilities in scale with existing buildings. Specifically, the GBQC plan laid out the rationale for a new Dining Hall Commons and

West Building

facilities for the School of Social Science (the West Building), both of which were to be sited west of Fuld Hall and north of the library. Once again Breuer was considered and rejected. Other contenders included Kevin Roche, Edward Larrabee Barnes, Richard Neutra, and Louis Kahn. But it was the dean of Princeton's School of Architecture, Robert Geddes, who ultimately won the commission. The complex he designed solved two different yet complementary issues: the West Building provided spacious offices and classroom space for the Schools of Historical Studies and Social Science, while the Dining Hall gave the Institute a much needed social and conference center.

In developing his design, Geddes enlisted the site as a silent (but eloquent) partner. When the new academic and social complex was first announced to be built immediately to the west of Fuld Hall, many resident faculty were opposed. The existing open, landscaped space was seen as a great amenity that would be swallowed up first by the construction and then the buildings themselves. Geddes' solution was to recast the challenge from an either/or issue to an accommodation of both: working hand in glove with the project landscape architects, Geddes made sure his design incorporated and celebrated the natural beauty of the site. So integral was the landscape that Geddes called it a clearing in the forest.

Like the library, its neighbor to the south, the Dining Hall and West Building make inspired use of the natural westward slope of the site. The slope allowed the architect to design a larger building than is at first apparent from the south campus. Because of the slope, the east cornice of the three-story building is level with the eave lines of the existing buildings. This has the further advantage of deferring to Fuld Hall, which remains the focus of the campus.

The Dining Hall and West Building are connected around garden courtyards into which the main dining hall, lounge, and private dining rooms open. The Commons provides facilities for seating 175 people in the main dining hall (furnished, incidentally, with Breuer's classic tubular and caneback chairs) and for 60 people in the private dining halls and board room. The exteriors of both buildings are predictably rectilinear and constructed of white trim, wood sash and panels, and unfinished concrete to reflect the texture, joints, and fasteners of the wooden mold into which the concrete was poured. The latter was a popular contemporary construction technique bordering on cliche.

Interior spaces work like no other building featured in this guide, largely because of the way in which the architect maximized the dramatic potential of the sloping site. Whether one enters from the front or back, the eye is caught by horizontal and vertical vistas through the complex. Multi-storied columns, massive concrete open stairways, balconies, ledges, and great expanses of glass suggest an Italian hilltown carved out of rock. The need for privacy as well as social interaction is deftly accommodated: like an Italian hilltown, the human presence can be inserted and easily rearranged as the need arises. In fact, Geddes consciously intended the modular planning to permit future adaptation. For the artful collaboration of the building's architect and the landscape architects, the project received an honor award from the Central New Jersey Chapter of the AIA in 1973.

100. Mathematics Building and Wolfensohn Hall

Cesar Pelli and Associates, 1993

The completion of the West Building and Dining Hall defined the western wall of the emerging south campus. The next obvious site for development was to the east, somewhere south of buildings "C" and "E." In fact, the 1968 Development Plan identified this as the location for a facility that would ultimately house the School of Mathematics. Like the West Building and Dining Hall complex, the result was two buildings: one that accommodated community functions, and the other designed for private, scholarly pursuits of residents. The buildings also anchored the southeast corner of the lower campus.

The program for this project addressed two issues: the need to gather all the mathematicians under one roof where they could interact, and the need for a large auditorium that could serve the Institute and also be a venue for the Princeton community. Pelli met both needs, and then some. The Mathematics Building included 48 offices and space for 85 scholars; Wolfensohn Hall yielded a 230-seat theater that could seat the entire Institute. The excellent acoustics identified Wolfensohn as a first-class concert hall for individual performers and small ensembles.

Pelli, 1995 recipient of the AIA's Gold Medal, takes his cue from Building "E." The Mathematics Building and Wolfensohn are likewise basically rectangles with the same east-west orientation as Building "E" to the north. With the siting of Wolfensohn, Pelli creates a court or loose quadrangle with Building "E," the focus of which is two large slabs of rock set to form a right angle. The rocks are in fact a fountain and a slate chalkboard. The chalkboard defines this place as the preserve of mathematicians, who communicate with one another through the medium of chalk and blackboards.

Here, too, the architect used a sloping site to accommodate buildings that are larger than they appear. The colonnade in front of the Mathematics Building and the arched truss in front of of Wolfensohn further enhance the ground-hugging nature of both, while offering abstract allusions to an older classical design tradition. The actual size of Wolfensohn and the Mathematics Building becomes clear as soon as one walks to the rear of both. Looking at the south elevation of the Mathematics Building reveals the ways in which Pelli manipulated the structure to break up what might otherwise have been an oppressively long wall.

Contemporary interviews with the project's designer, Jeff Paine, indicate that the users—the mathematicians—had few but very specific wishes regarding the interior: comfort; no distractions; opportunities for interaction with colleagues; and blackboards. In response to the request for a peaceful environment with a minimum of visual or auditory distractions, the architects specified fabrics with muted tones and blonde oak throughout. To accommodate opportunities for interaction, they designed wide, well-lit halls and stairways where the fellows could pause for easy conversation. A footnote on the blackboards: these are real slate, recycled from old school buildings.

The Mathematics Building may make glancing allusions to older, historic forms, but it is Wolfensohn Hall that resonates with an ancient past.

Wolfensohn Hall and Mathematics Building

The front entrance is sheltered by a wooden arched truss that rests at each edge on round pillars. The prototype seems to be the temple, a classic public building, with the truss serving as the tympanum. Certainly the entrance is appropriately dramatic for a performance space. It also provides predator-free perches for roosting birds, an unexpected visual dimension to the experience of entering the foyer..

Inside the auditorium, the clean space features curving wall panels of red cherry wood, which ensures rich and resonant sound. This care for the quality of the acoustics is carried up to the ceiling, which continues the pattern of arched wood trusses first seen outside. Acoustical consultants ruled out the flat gypsum board and metal truss ceiling that had been initially proposed. A measure of the hall's excellence: violinist Isaac Stern performed the inaugural concert in April 1993.

101. Bloomberg Hall

Robert Geddes and Kehrt Shatken Sharon Architects, 2000

With the opening of the Wolfensohn Hall and the Math Building complex, the Institute claimed state-of-the-art facilities for three of its four schools. In addition to the administration building, there was now a library, a social center, and a performance or assembly hall. As the Institute approached its seventieth anniversary, the unfinished work was a home for the School of Natural Sciences, some of whose resident scholars are currently posted in Building "D." Their new home will be Bloomberg Hall. A bird's eye view of the main campus reveals that the east side is still loosely defined between Buildings "C" and "E." The new home for the School of Natural Sciences will link "C" and "E" with an L-shaped glass addition. The brick addition will feature a common room with floor-to-ceiling glass on both north and south elevations, topped (budget permitting) by a copper roof. As for Building "D," which will be vacated, plans call for a complete renovation to house the Institute's newest scholarly endeavor, the Program in Theoretical Biology.

Princeton Borough

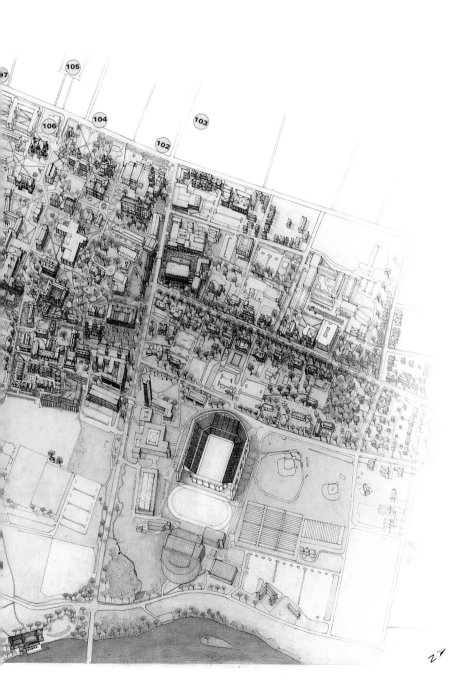

Princeton is a wonderful little spot, a quaint and ceremonious village.
— Albert Einstein, November 20, 1933

In 1896, when the College of New Jersey became Princeton University, it chose to honor the community in which it resided. Other American colleges have changed their names in rising to university status, but not to their placenames : King's College became Columbia University; Queens College to Rutgers; and the College of Rhode Island became Brown University. In spite of coming into this town-gown marriage willingly, having offered the land required to attract the College of New Jersey to relocate there from Newark, the borough of Princeton has had times of misunderstandings and even fights with the school, especially when the university is perceived to be throwing its weight around. Yet both have prospered and continue to draw strength from the other. The shared name underscores the family resemblance and shared destiny.

Evidence of the tie between the two appears in the buildings of the community. Architects such as Steadman, Notman, and Gildersleeve worked in both. Alumni such as Moses Taylor Pyne and Edgar Palmer used their money and influence to shape the town in ways they believed would enhance the university. And there are the local materials of brick and stone that reinforce the visual continuity between the campus and the town. There is likewise similar architectural styles, from Georgian to modern, which infuse in the university and the town an authentic variety and liveliness that other towns and neighborhoods would envy. There is here little of the artificial pickling of historic buildings that in many communities passes for a preservation ethic. Ultimately the most powerful force for convergence is no doubt the simple fact that much of the land on both sides of Nassau Street has belonged to or been controlled by the Princeton University at one time or another over two hundred years.

All of which is to state the obvious: Nassau Street, the main street, has two sides. It is a permeable byway that fosters a town–gown dialogue that continues to shape both. And so this guide ends where the university began—with the town that gave it the means for its future. This Walk along Nassau Street and around the adjoining neighborhood makes no pretense at being complete. The author will leave to the reader a more leisurely engagement with the town, and simply suggest points of departure.

Bainbridge House

102. Bainbridge House, 158 Nassau Street   *circa 1755–1760*

Bainbridge House is the logical first stop, since it is one of the oldest buildings on the north side of Nassau Street and headquarters of the Historical
Society of Princeton. Built by Job Stockton, a wealthy tanner, the house
honors the memory of an early resident, Commodore William Bainbridge,
the commander of Old Ironsides during the War of 1812. It is one of few
remaining eighteenth-century houses in Princeton Borough, and presents
obvious stylistic affinities to the university's Maclean House. Both were
among the first structures to use brick as a facing material. What distinguishes Bainbridge House from Maclean House on the south side of Nassau
Street is a greater fidelity to the original Georgian design. The crisp articulation of the design elements of Bainbridge, for example, is lost when the
brick is painted as it is on Maclean. Also, the roof of Maclean was raised
and a porch added; one has to look at Bainbridge to understand how
Maclean looked when it was first built. Some of Bainbridge's historic interior is intact, including the original paneled walls in the second-floor main
room and the staircase. Also inside is a treasured collection of artifacts and
history about the town. The university owns Bainbridge House, and leases it
to the historical society for an annual fee of one dollar.

Beatty House

103. Beatty House, 19 Vandeventer Avenue *circa 1780*

Beatty House, around the corner, is also owned by the Princeton Historical Society. It too is another instance of peripatetic preservation, having been moved in 1875 from a site on the south side of Nassau Street (approximately where Firestone Library now stands) to this location. The graceful arched fanlight over the front door and the flanking side lights as well as the raised keystone lintels of the front windows are hallmarks of a transition from heavy Georgian design to the more delicate Federal style. Inside, the focus of the parlor is the splendid early-nineteenth-century mantelpiece, skillfully executed with garlands of wheat, laboring farmers, and putti with field implements to celebrate Princeton's agricultural origins.

104. Lower Pyne, 92 Nassau Street
  Raleigh C. Gildersleeve, 1896

Back on the north side of Nassau Street, this time headed west, is the half-timbered Tudor revival landmark called Lower Pyne, the surviving twin of a pair of undergraduate dormitories commissioned by Moses Taylor Pyne '77. The year in which this structure was built—1896, the university's sesquicentennial—offers an important clue as to what Pyne was up to. This is the watershed year when Princeton's trustees mandated Collegiate Gothic as the official style. Pyne was perhaps the most vociferous advocate. Inspired by the same spirit transforming the university, of which he was a leading light, Pyne sought to recast the north side of Nassau Street as a more appropriate setting for the "Oxbridge" institution taking shape to the south, or, as he put it, "to bring a touch of English living to a growing college town." If the university was to be America's new Cambridge, Nassau should be an English "High Street." Indeed, Pyne sent a college employee to study the residence-over-commercial buildings in Oxford and Cambridge; then conveyed the information and commission to Gildersleeve, his favorite architect. The upper floors of both dormitories, which Pyne gave to the university, housed twenty students each, while the ground floor was rented out to

Lower Pyne

commercial tenants. It may be hokey, but a recent careful restoration reveals a handsome structure that contributes mightily to the visual variety of the street. The students have long since retreated to the other side of the FitzRandolph Gates. Upper Pyne has been demolished and Lower Pyne sold in 1985 to a British-owned real estate company. The two precincts remain zoned off from one another to this day.

105. Palmer Square *Thomas Stapleton, 1936–1939; Charles K. Agle, 1963–1964*

Edgar Palmer '03, another influential Princeton alumnus, also tried his hand at redesigning Nassau Street. As he saw it, the town lacked a municipal focus. Had Princeton been the seat of government, it might have been orga-nized around a legislative hall; had religion played a central role as it did in many New England colonies, Princeton might have grown around a church and a commons. Instead, the town's design was dictated by the fact that it was a stop along the King's Highway between New York City and Philadelphia. This street was the focus. Pyne had dressed the street in English garb; Palmer, the heir to a zinc fortune, had larger ambitions and set out to create a municipal campus center in the heart of town.

The need for such a center had been anticipated by the work of the Architectural Improvement Society of Princeton, a semi-independent associ-ation committed to preserving "Princeton's character as an attractive place of residence." The group raised money as early as 1924 to hire a profes-sional town planner and in 1925 recommended the building of a plaza that would eventually be Palmer Square. But the national Depression inter-vened. When Edgar Palmer infused new life into the project in the mid-

Palmer Square

1930s, it reflected the then contemporary celebration of Americana, such as the re-creation of Colonial Williamsburg, also influencing painting, movies, and music of the period.

Stapleton created Palmer Square by punching a hole through the existing grid, and inserting a village green—surrounded to the west by small-scaled colonial revival buildings. Nassau Tavern, rather than a church or a government building, anchored the green. In the course of its migration from its previous location on Nassau Street to Palmer Green, the *Tavern* was re-christened a much more tony *Inn*. Ironically, Stapleton's plan was implemented by moving out a number of Princeton's historic houses, as well as poor and minority families who lived there. World War II interrupted full realization of Stapleton's neocolonial plan, and when work resumed in the 1960s on the east side, it was animated by a different spirit.

The new architect, Charles K. Agle (1906–1988), shelved Stapleton's colonial revival plan and substituted a single five-story (six stories at the back), L-shaped brick structure with punched windows and a hip roof. Sacrificed in the process was Upper Pyne, the other half of Gildersleeve's half-timbered Tudor Revival project on Nassau Street. But that was not the only loss. The large brick box that was built on the east side of Palmer Square makes the obvious point that it is usually cheaper to build one structure with large open-floor interiors than a series of smaller ones. Such a structure is also less expensive to heat and clean, thus more profitable to lease. Construction costs are likewise lowered on a per square foot basis the higher the developer builds. What a community, including Princeton, typically got in the 1960s for permitting the extra height and bulk was a windswept plaza. This is what today occupies Nassau Street like a beached whale.

For the pedestrian, Agle's office building is inferior to the Palmer Square of the 1930s. The windows and doorways on the earlier, west side of the square, for example, follow the land as it slopes away from Nassau Street; the later east side fights the grade. Compare how light and shadow play on the windows of both. The neocolonial ambiance of Palmer Square West is admittedly ersatz, but it is certainly preferable to the bloated fortress on the other side. It does not help that the architect tricks up the office building by applying traditional features (the hipped roof and projecting eaves). Stuck on to what is at heart a modern office building, they are inappropriate and totally out of scale. The economics of modern real estate may award the palm to the office building, but charm, character, and human scale are the permanent residents of the buildings to the west.

106. Nassau Presbyterian Church (formerly First Presbyterian Church) *Thomas U. Walter, 1835*

Nassau Presbyterian Church

Across from Palmer Square on the south side of the street stands the dignified Greek Revival facade of Nassau Presbyterian Church, by Thomas U. Walter (1804–1887). It was the architect of the Seminary's Miller Chapel, Charles Steadman, Princeton's premiere carpenter-builder-architect, who had commissioned Walter to design the project. Steadman was also its chief underwriter. Buying a design from an architect and then building it oneself was a common practice at the time. However, Steadman's contribution was hardly passive; he laid out the interior and was responsible for the excellent construction.

The leading American architect of his day, Walter came to his profession naturally as the son and grandson of Philadelphia builders. He rapidly established himself in what was then the design center of America, ultimately winning a competition in 1850 for the extension of the United States Capitol in Washington, D.C. He is perhaps best known for his design of the Capitol's great cast-iron dome.

Although the church is an early work by Walter, it conveys the confidence of a knowledgeable craftsman. The absence of windows at the front draws the eye to the over-scaled, recessed porch, an effect augmented by the two massive Ionic columns that frame the line of sight of passers by. At once delicate and strong, open and screened off, the entrance irresistibly draws those on the street into a realm intended to be apart from the bustle of university and town. Walter's refined design widely influenced American church architecture well into the twentieth century. Until the construction of Alexander Hall in 1892, most of Princeton College's commencement exercises were held here.

Over the years, the church (with the permission of the university, which owns the surrounding property) has built a series of five major additions, the most recent (1988) by the Princeton firm of Short and Ford. A complete record of how the building has expanded is captured on a drawing by Short and Ford that hangs in the hall outside the sanctuary. In theory, it should have been virtually impossible to accommodate any additions to Walter's tight classical form. Yet in practice the church congregation has been careful to commission work that has never compromised the powerful presence Walter's design continues to exert on the street.

107. Princeton Bank and Trust Company, 12–14 Nassau Street *W. E. Stone, 1896*

Princeton Bank and Trust Co.

Curious and certainly the most delightful commercial building in town is the old Princeton Bank and Trust Company. No apologies have to be made for the affection Victorians had for revivalist styles when such gingerbread playfulness is the result. The architect apparently understood that people buy more and profits rise when an element of the theatrical is introduced to the commercial realm. The same impulse is appreciated by modern retailers who apply holiday decorations to the warehouse boxes of suburban shopping malls. Here the decoration is not cosmetic; it is bred in the bone.

The Dutch Baroque design may harken back to New Jersey's past as a Dutch colony. Whatever the impetus, Stone's reinterpretation of Haarlem's seventeenth-century meat market announces the start of the commercial district. The polychrome brickwork, the corbiestep gable at the front, the projecting surrounds of the upper story windows, the pagoda-like finials, and undulating pediment—all are the tectonic fireworks of a master-builder celebrating the 150th anniversary of the town's most distinguished resident.

108. Palmer House, Nassau Street and Bayard Lane

Charles Steadman, 1823

Charles Steadman's name comes up in most conversations about Princeton architecture, for this is a nineteenth-century town. A carpenter, architect, contractor, and developer, Steadman was a one-stop operator who did not confuse convenience with expediency. Approximately 40 of the more than 70 buildings attributed to him survive. Although hardly innovative, his residential designs were distinguished by consistent quality. Albert Einstein lived in a Steadman house (originally located on Alexander Street but moved to 112 Mercer Street) and the official residence of the Governor of New Jersey is a Steadman design, arguably his most luxurious (Drumthwacket, 1835, 354 Stockton Street; formerly the home of Moses Taylor Pyne). Mixing Federal elements (the arched fanlight over the entry, for example) with the newer taste for Greek Revival (the exterior columns and pilasters as well as the higher ceilings inside), Steadman created a hybrid, which like a good hybrid combined the strengths of both parents. Unlike Georgian houses, which characteristically offer a rectangular unpainted brick facade with a steeply-pitched roof, Palmer House shows its Greek Revival roots in its square facade, the easing of the roof pitch and the painting of the exterior brick (or wood) white to suggest marble.

Steadman's client was a member of one of the community's first families, Robert Stockton III, who commissioned the house for his Charleston bride. Over time, the house has been enlarged to serve the changing needs of its occupants, but the front is essentially that which Steadman designed. In the twentieth century the property was bought by Edgar Palmer, whose widow donated the house to the university. Having painted it a buttery yellow, Princeton uses it to house guests.

109. Princeton Battle Monument, Nassau Street at Bayard Lane and Stockton Street

Carrère & Hastings, architect; Frederick MacMonnies, sculptor, 1922

The great monument at the head of Nassau Street commemorates a significant moment in the history of the town, the university, and the nation—the decisive Revolutionary battle of January 3, 1777. The monument was an idea many years in the making. MacMonnies (1863–1937), a Brooklyn-born sculptor working in France, had been awarded the commission in 1908. He proposed a giant relief on a pylon. Anyone who has visited Paris will note an uncanny resemblance to the sculpted piers on the Arc de Triomphe. Until the period after the First World War, fairly literal copies of designs of other artists and architects was more likely to be seen as a mark of sophistication than plagiarism. The architect and sculptor of the monument only needed

Princeton Battle Monument

to look across the street at the Oxbridge profile of the university's new Holder complex to confirm that when it came to imitation they were in good company.

MacMonnies' initial design did not sit well with the clients. As a result, the Battle Monument Commission required MacMonnies to collaborate with an architect. He knew Thomas Hastings (1860–1929) from the Ecole des Beaux-Arts in Paris, had worked with him since, and proposed they collaborate. The sculpture depicts General Washington leading his troops into the Battle of Princeton, as well as the death of General Hugh Mercer.

Near Nassau Street

Einstein's "quaint and ceremonious village" encompasses more than Nassau Street. The reader who has followed this guide as far as the Battle Monument can retrace his or her steps back to the center of the borough or take a more circuitous route that passes by other nearby buildings of architectural or historic interest.

110. Morven, 55 Stockton Street *circa 1755, 1848*

Morven

Morven was built by Richard Stockton II, a signer of the Declaration of Independence, and named after the mythical home of Fingal in McPherson's eighteenth-century literary hoax, *The Poems of Ossian*. At one time the official residence of the State Governor, Morven is in essence Georgian. But it has been renovated and restored so extensively that little of the original structure remains— apart from the plan, walls, and major partitions. Even in its altered condition, Morven defines the moment when Princeton was no longer a frontier settlement, but a cultivated seat capable of dispensing gracious hospitality.

111. Trinity Church, 33 Mercer Street

Richard M. Upjohn, 1868; Ralph Adams Cram renovation, 1914–1915;
interior remodeling, 1963

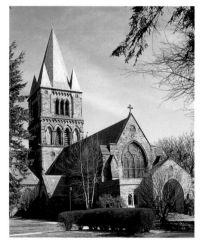

Trinity Church

Charles Steadman designed and built the first home for the newly organized Episcopal congregation in Princeton (no longer extant). Not surprisingly, it was a Greek stone temple fronted by a portico of six wooden columns. Torn down in 1868 and replaced by a Gothic Revival edifice more in keeping with the liturgical practices of the Anglican client, the second Trinity Church was designed by Richard M. Upjohn (1828–1903), son of the eminent architect of New York's Trinity Church and one of the founders of The American Institute of Architects. Old photographs suggest that the building Upjohn designed was rather squat. When the vestry decided to enlarge the church, they engaged Princeton's supervising architect, Ralph Adams Cram. Cram used the opportunity to redesign a more graceful structure, which was in part accomplished by heightening the steeple. Being more liturgically precise than Upjohn, Cram relocated the entrance from the south to the west (the setting sun, death; the rising sun, life). A devastating fire in 1963 created the opportunity to reorient the sanctuary consistent with contemporary liturgical innovations. The altar was moved forward in front of the pulpit and lectern, and the choir was relocated to the back of the sanctuary.

112. Ivy Hall, 43 Mercer Street   *John Notman, 1846*

Initially built to house Princeton's abortive attempt to create a law school, Ivy has served a wide array of occupants, from the office of the Delaware and Raritan Canal Company to the home of the College's first Eating Club. Today, the building is owned by Trinity Church. Although a small building, it is distinguished by big architecture, from the tall openings of the triple-arched portico to skillful handling of the stone masonry.

113. House, 34 Edgehill Street   *circa 1840*

House, 34 Edgehill Street

No record of the architect seems to survive, but the Greek Revival style indicates it was built around 1840. This house was unusual for Princeton, since builders typically used the temple form only for churches and other public buildings, rather than private residences. The high quality of the carpentry reflected Princeton's affluence at the time, at least up to the national financial panic of 1837. Already somewhat dated for its time, this house marked the end of Princeton's rich Greek Revival phase.

114. The Barracks   *Richard Stockton, 1696*

The Barracks

Just down the street stands one of Princeton's oldest houses. The ceiling beams in the basement are made of undressed tree trunks, but there is more evidence of the structure's long history. The orientation away from Edgehill Street reveals that the house existed before Princeton had a defined street grid. As the Stockton family grew and prospered, it simply added to existing elements, incorporating them into a larger design. This was common practice in Princeton, which typically resulted in houses that appeared to be constructed like trains, each generation adding a different car—a wing arranged in a straight line along the front rather than perpendicularly to the rear. An easy though not fool-proof clue to the age of a particular section is the ceiling height: the lower the ceiling, the greater the age. Standing in front of the Barracks shows that the right wing and the entry are modern additions. Because each succeeding generation of the Stockton family continued to use the local stone of the original, the house has a certain unity it might otherwise lack. The Barracks name came from the hated practice of billeting soldiers in private houses during the French and Indian Wars (1755–1760).

Mercer Street

115. Mercer Street

At this point, the most direct route back to the university is to turn left on
Mercer Street. A stroll down Mercer with a turn right into Alexander Street
is an opportunity to experience how urban design evolves. Most of the
buildings are by Charles Steadman and they tend to follow a similar form:
two stories, three bays, an off-center entrance, and clapboard exteriors
painted uniformly white. It might be monotonous, but it is not. No two
entrances were designed quite alike: from the fanlights, the capitals, the
omnipresent pillars. Steadman likewise varied the cornices. There is privacy, but there is also neighborhood. It is light years ahead of the current
wave of MacMansions being built on half-acre lots around the country.
Steadman and his contemporaries were not building monuments; they
were instead building communities. It is this legacy more than any one
great building that distinguishes every precinct of "this wonderful little
spot, [this] quaint and ceremonious village."

Epilogue

In the *Death and Life of Great American Cities,* writer Jane Jacobs described urban environments as organic forms that, like creatures of nature, experience a cycle of growth, maturity, and inevitabley decay. Sometimes that decay is caused by a natural tendency toward entropy. But often decline and decay are the unintended consequences of success. A place as attractive as Princeton can be all too easily overwhelmed by those who love it, driving up real estate prices and creating a congestion that finally strangles what inspired love in the first place. The citizens of Princeton and its institutions strive for a dynamic equilibrium, sometimes together, sometimes at cross-purposes. The future of Princeton, the town and the institutions it has nourished and who nourish it, depends on maintaining a delicate, dynamic balance. Whether Princeton can escape the destructive force of human nature is a story still being written and the subject of other commentaries.

Balmori, Diana, Diane Kostial McGuire, Eleanor M. McPeck. *Beatrix Farrand's American Landscapes: Her Gardens & Campuses.* Sagaponack, NY: Sagapress, 1985.

Beatrix Jones Farrand (1872–1959): Fifty Years of American Landscape Architecture . Washington, D.C.: Dumbarton Oaks, Trustees for Harvard University, 1982. Eighth Dumbarton Oaks Colloquium on the History of Landscape Architecture, Washington, D.C., 1980.

Breese, Gerald. *Princeton University Land: 1752–1984.* Princeton, NJ: Princeton University Press, 1986.

Campus: Guide to Princeton University. Princeton, NJ: Princeton University Office of Communications, 1997.

Evans, William K. *Princeton: A Picture Postcard History of Princeton and Princeton University.* Vestal, NY: Almar Press, 1993.

Gambee, Robert. *Princeton.* New York: W. W. Norton, 1998.

Greiff, Constance M., Mary W. Gibbons, and Elizabeth G. C. Menzies. *Princeton Architecture: A Pictorial History of Town and Campus.* Princeton, NJ: Princeton University Press, 1967.

Lane, Wheaton J., editor. *Pictorial History of Princeton.* Princeton, NJ: Princeton University Press, 1947.

Larson, Jens Fredrick. *Architectural Planning of the American College.* New York, 1933.

Leitch, Alexander. A Princeton Companion. Princeton, NJ: Princeton University Press, 1978.

Oberdorfer, Don. *Princeton University: The First 250 Years.* Princeton, NJ: Princeton University Press, 1995.

Princeton University. *An Interactive Campus History: 1746–1996.* A virtual walk through the Princeton campus. http//mondrian.princeton.edu.

Selden, William K. *Club Life at Princeton.* Princeton, NJ: Princeton Prospect Foundation, 1994.

———. *The Legacy of John Cleve Green.* Princeton, NJ: Princeton University, 1988.

———. *Nassau Hall.* Princeton, NJ: Princeton University, 1995.

———. *Princeton Theological Seminary: A Narrative History 1812–1992.* Princeton, NJ: Princeton University Press, 1992.

Shand-Tucci, Douglass. *Boston Bohemia: 1881–1900.* Amherst, MA: University of Massachusetts Press, 1995.

Short, William H. and Constance M. Greiff. "Small Town, Distinguished Architects." Parts 1 and 2. *Princeton History, The Journal of the Historical Society of Princeton,* no. 8 (1989) and no. 9 (1990).

Thorp, Willard, Minor Myers Jr., and Jeremiah Stanton Finch. *The Princeton Graduate School: A History.* Princeton, NJ: Princeton University Press, 1978.

Turner, Paul Venable. *Campus: An American Planning Tradition.* Cambridge, MA: MIT Press, 1990.

Wertenbaker, Thomas Jefferson. *Princeton: 1746–1896.* Princeton, NJ: Princeton University Press, 1996. Preface by John M. Murrin.

Acknowledgments

Acknowledgments are built on a paradox: most readers skip over these pages; yet for those who linger no section is more closely read. Which leads me to say to all those I may (unintentionally) omit, be assured the debt I owe you is felt even if it is not noted in print.

Among the first order of angels must surely be the men and women who gave the walks in this guide their shape. Absent the architects, engineers, landscape architects, carpenters, masons, and every member of each building team, there would be no book. Likewise, the author is indebted to the trustees, administrators, faculty, and alumni of Princeton University, as well as of the collateral institutions of higher learning. Theirs was the vision, passion, and financial resources that dreams are made of.

Next is the debt owed to those who have written perceptively about the university and the larger community of which it is the center and a part. The work of Constance Greiff and her various collaborators is as delightful as it is intelligent. Clear and eminently sensible, Greiff weaves the history and architecture of town and gown into a compelling tapestry. The late Gerald Breese's investigation into the university's acquisition of land offers an insight into how a combination of foresight and luck has given Princeton the room to grow while protecting the area from inappropriate development. Paul Venable Turner's pioneering study of planning at America's colleges is essential to grasping how and why the campus is a unique American form to be treasured.

To this list must be added the students and faculty who contributed to the creation of Princeton's Mondrian Project. Always informative, often witty, and refreshingly anecdotal, the project is an inspired cyberspace tour of a virtual campus just a browser and a monitor away from any desktop in the world. At the other extreme of technology is William Evans' collection of historic postcards, an absolutely first-rate and novel way of researching Princeton's architectural past. Finally, there are the numerous publications by William K. Selden. Whether he is writing about the eating clubs of Prospect Avenue, the legacy of a generous donor, or the history of Princeton Theological Seminary, Selden puts a welcome human face on his subjects.

Princeton University's superb library system was a joy to me as a graduate student in the late 1960s. Now, years later, one of the system's repositories, the Seeley G. Mudd Manuscript Library, proved to be an invaluable resource for archival materials about the University's architecture. The comfortable surroundings and the uniformly helpful staff were as treasured in their way as the unparalleled holdings themselves. A similar spirit prevailed at the library of the Institute for Advanced Study, which is housed in one of the most luminous research facilities in which this writer has ever worked. In particular, I would like to thank Librarian Marcia Tucker and Archival Assistant Lisa Coats for going the extra mile to lighten my work. In the borough of Princeton, the Historical Society of Princeton, housed in one of the oldest buildings on Nassau Street, is a small facility with a big mission. Particular thanks go to Maureen Smyth for offering warm comfort on a bitterly cold winter day.

Of the many who guided and encouraged me, there is a special honor roll reserved for those who despite their busy schedules generously gave me their time. At the university, there is first and foremost Ben Kessler, whose encyclopedic knowledge of Princeton is one of the living treasures on campus. I also received assistance from Jon D. Hlafter, Director of Physical Planning at the University. Mary Caffrey, Senior Writer in Princeton's Office of Communications and Publications, worked more efficiently in producing a new child than I did writing this guide and still had the time to give me much needed help. At the Seminary, the Librarian for Archives and Special Collections, Reverend William Harris, offered the sort of gentle encouragement that reminded me of the best of my undergraduate and graduate professors. It was Harris who introduced me to William Selden, who kindly answered questions that in retrospect were often naive. In the face of the relative dearth of printed materials on the Institute for Advanced Study, I am especially indebted to its Assistant Director, Allen Rowe, for the time he took by phone and email to open doors for my research. Jim Gatsch, AIA, and Michael Mills, AIA, of the Princeton architectural firm Ford Farewell Mills & Gatsch offered me the names and telephone numbers of what proved to be indispensable human resources, some of whom I have already acknowledged.

A special burden was placed on those to whom I turned for honest reactions to the drafts I turned out. Among these, I want to single out Michael J. Stanton, FAIA, the 1999 American Institute of Architects president, Heather Ewing, Richard Van Os Keuls, Melissa Houghton of The American Architectural Foundation, and George Hartman, FAIA. Their suggestions were always well intended—and, more often than not, they saved me from an awkward turn of phrase or an outright mistake.

Nor can I omit thanking former AIA Executive Vice President/ CEO Mark Hurwitz and his successor, Norman Koonce, FAIA. Both respected the fact that I was deep into this book, sometimes at the expense of a work assignment, yet quietly gave me their full support, even looking the other way when I slipped off to the AIA's library to do some research.

Which brings me to those who are directly associated with the production of this book. First, to my publisher, Kevin Lippert, my gratitude and respect for the contribution the Princeton Architectural Press is making to an appreciation of the design achievement of America's colleges and universities. A sincere thank you as well to Jane Garvie, map maker extraordinaire, whose three-dimensional aerial maps of the campus are an equal mixture of clarity and delight. The design layout of a publication is a more subtle art that nevertheless profoundly affects a book's reception; here, both the reader and the author are indebted to Sara Stemen.

My editor Jan Cigliano gave me the opportunity to take up this project. Part nursemaid, part stern taskmistress, she had the responsibility of untying some of my knottier prose, for which readers owe her their own gratitude. Finally, my collaborator and partner, this guide's photographer, Walter Smalling. When my own confidence faltered, he had confidence for two. When he was not dealing with the vagaries of light and impossible-to-shoot-camera angles, he was a discerning sounding board not afraid to tell me I was all wet. This book is truly a child for which we have joint custody. I can vouch for the beauty of his contribution. The rest is just words.

Raymond P. Rhinehart
Washington, D.C.